Strength Training for FOOTBALL

Bruno Pauletto, MS
University of Tennessee

Human Kinetics Publishers

Library of Congress Cataloging-in-Publication Data

Pauletto, Bruno, 1954-
    Strength training for football / Bruno Pauletto.
      p.   cm.
    ISBN 0-87322-398-5
    1. Weight training. 2. Football. I. Title.
  GV546.P297 1993
  613.7′13--dc20   92-12982
                                                        CIP

ISBN: 0-87322-398-5

Exercise and health are matters that vary from individual to individual. Readers should speak with their own doctors about their individual needs before starting any strength-training program. This book is not intended as a substitute for the medical advice and supervision of your personal physician. Any application of the recommendations set forth in the following pages is at the reader's discretion and sole risk.

Note. Some of the photos in this book originally appeared in Strength Training for Coaches, copyright 1991 by Bruno Pauletto. They are reprinted by permission.

Acquisitions Editor: Brian Holding
Managing Editor: Julia Anderson
Assistant Editor: Dawn Roselund
Copyeditor: Jane Bowers
Proofreader: Tom Rice
Production Director: Ernie Noa
Typesetter: Julie Overholt
Text Design: Keith Blomberg
Text Layout: Tara Welsch
Cover Photo: Dave Black
Interior Photos: Nick Myers
Models: David Hawkins, William Hudson
Printer: United Graphics

Human Kinetics books are available at special discounts for bulk purchase for sales promotions, premiums, fund-raising, or educational use. Special editions or book excerpts can also be created to specification. For details, contact the Special Sales Manager at Human Kinetics.

Printed in the United States of America

10 9 8 7 6 5 4 3 2

Human Kinetics Publishers
Box 5076, Champaign, IL 61825-5076
1-800-747-4457

Canada Office:
Human Kinetics Publishers
P.O. Box 2503, Windsor, ON N8Y 4S2
1-800-465-7301 (in Canada only)

Europe Office:
Human Kinetics Publishers (Europe) Ltd.
P.O. Box IW14
Leeds LS16 6TR
England
0532-781708

Australia Office:
Human Kinetics Publishers
P.O. Box 80
Kingswood 5062
South Australia 374-0433

To Jesus Christ, my personal savior

Contents

Foreword

Much of our success in the football program at the University of Tennessee can be traced to the fact that we are working with stronger and faster athletes. The man behind our strength program is Bruno Pauletto.

Bruno has been instrumental in our football program for 15 years. Since his addition to our staff as the strength and conditioning coach, we have seen great improvement in the strength, flexibility, agility, quickness, and overall conditioning of our players. The general improvement in muscular strength has also helped reduce the number and seriousness of injuries.

Our football players are involved in a year-round weight training program, much like the one presented in this book. I am convinced that this program has made each member of our team a better player and has given us a stronger team.

Now Bruno Pauletto is putting his expertise into print to help other football players perform better. The program presented in this book can be individualized for every player—it's designed to help you make improvements where you need them most. By following this program you should increase your total body strength, a basic first step to becoming a better football player.

Johnny Majors
Head Football Coach
University of Tennessee

About the Author

Bruno Pauletto is a nationally recognized authority in strength and conditioning education and a former Olympian. In his various capacities as president of the National Strength and Conditioning Association and strength and conditioning coach at the University of Tennessee, Knoxville, Pauletto realizes that strength training is much more than pumping iron. It is a well-planned, systematic process designed to improve total body strength.

Pauletto holds an MS in physical education with an emphasis in exercise physiology from the University of Tennessee, Knoxville (UTK). He is a certified strength and conditioning specialist and a member of the National Football Coaches Association. He has also coordinated strength-training programs for men's varsity athletics at UTK and conducts annual strength clinics throughout the United States.

Preface

During my 15 years as strength and conditioning coach at the University of Tennessee, I have had the privilege and opportunity to coach several football players who have gone on to great success in the NFL. I have seen how a well-planned strength-training program has helped them to reach high levels of performance. Throughout my coaching career, I have developed a year-round strength-training program for football players and now have put it on paper for you to use. I have found this program to be very effective in training my players and hope you will be able to use it to become a better football player.

This book was written for you, the football player. It contains the information you need to perform a safe and efficient strength program to help you play better. Whether you play football at the junior high, high school, or college level, this book can help you.

Strength training is much more than just ''pumping iron.'' It is a well-planned, systematic process designed to improve total body strength. Increased strength will make you run faster, jump higher, and tackle with more force. It will also reduce your chance of injury.

This book not only explains what you need to do but also takes you step-by-step through a full year of specific workouts. The book is divided into three parts.

Part I, ''Maximizing Your Strength Potential,'' opens with chapter 1, ''Strength Concerns for Football,'' which discusses the importance of strength for football players. It also addresses the relationship of different playing positions and their specific strength requirements. The factors involved in increasing muscle mass (bulking up) are also explained.

Chapter 2, ''Strength-Training Guidelines,'' contains information you need to know before you begin your program. Read this chapter thoroughly as it will make the rest of the book easier to understand.

Chapter 3, ''Designing Your Own Program,'' shows you how to evaluate your present strength level and how to set starting weights for each exercise. This chapter also explains the importance of setting and reaching your goals, which are basic to any successful weight program.

Chapter 4, ''Starting Your Program,'' explains each training cycle, its approximate duration, and its purpose. This chapter also includes instructions for completing your workout plan using the charts in this book. A section on testing tells you how to determine if you've met your goals. The chapter ends with information to help you if you fall short of reaching your goals.

Part II, ''The Yearly Workout Plan,'' consists of chapters 5, 6, 7, and 8. These chapters provide charts for your daily training logs for the entire year. Each day's log shows the exercises to be done, the number of sets and reps, and how heavy you should lift. Both a split routine (lift 4 days per week) and a total-body routine (lift 3 days per week) are presented. You choose the routine that works best for you.

The third part of the book, ''Strength-Training Exercises,'' is devoted entirely to the exercises you'll be doing. Chapter 9 shows the core exercises with photographs and basic instructions for how to do them correctly. Chapter 10 gives instructions for how to do the auxiliary exercises.

The appendixes contain the charts you will need to modify the program to suit your strength level: a strength-training percentages table, core and auxiliary exercise weight progression tables, and a personal best conversion chart. The glossary at the end of the book defines terms that you may not be familiar with.

Acknowledgments

Thanks to my wife, Julie, whose support, dedication, and hard work helped make this book possible.

- Thanks also to my many coaching friends throughout the country who through the years have helped broaden my experience in the field;
- the staff at Human Kinetics Publishers;
- photographer Nick Myers for a job well done; and
- models David Hawkins and William Hudson.

MAXIMIZING YOUR STRENGTH POTENTIAL

CHAPTER 1

Strength Concerns for Football

As you well know, a football player has to be strong. If your opponent has similar skill, speed, and conditioning but you are significantly stronger, you will be superior on the field.

But what you might not know is how to get the most strength gains out of your workouts. Every strength program needs a plan and a goal. This book gives you a plan for a full year of workouts and tells you how to execute it to reach your goals. By dedicating yourself to improvement and following my guidelines, you will see your body get stronger.

You strengthen your body to improve your performance, but strength also reduces the chance of injury. The better prepared your body is to run, block, and tackle, the lower your chance of injury.

There are various ways to get stronger. None is absolutely better than the others. The training program (exercises, sets, repetitions, loads) I suggest is what I have found to be effective. Your genetic makeup and motivation will be the deciding factors in how strong you get.

TOTAL BODY STRENGTH

The program presented here is designed to improve your total body strength. Whichever position you play, total body strength is necessary. You might think that because you play a particular position, your strength program should differ from that of an athlete who plays another position (for example, quarterback vs. offensive line). This is partly true; let me explain. Before doing specific exercises or special training, you need several years of basic strength-training experience and good overall strength. Position-specific training will be of little help otherwise. The program in this book will develop that basic overall strength that all football players need, regardless of position.

If you have been strength training for several years and your body is well developed, you can add some position-specific exercises to your basic program. The workout pages of this book have spaces for you and your coach to add specific exercises that you think are important to your needs.

Although strength training improves your physical ability to play your position, it does not improve your skill. Practice is the key to improving the skill itself. For example, a stronger arm can help a quarterback throw harder and farther, but only through practice can he develop the precision and proper execution necessary to complete the passes.

BULKING UP

When muscles are strength-trained, they get bigger. How much bigger varies greatly from one athlete to another. For example, some athletes are linemen; they have large frames and big muscles. Wide receivers have a much smaller body structure. The bigger athlete who has a larger frame and can lift heavier weights will gain more muscle mass than a smaller athlete who uses a similar workout. This works out well because linemen need more bulk than other players. Whatever your size, you can improve your playing performance through strength training.

Muscle mass gain, or *bulking up*, is affected by the following:

1. Genetics is a major factor in how big or strong you can become.
2. Proper training techniques and dedication to improvement are important.
3. True bulking up is gaining muscle, not fat. Gaining fat will not help you become a better football player, but gaining muscle mass will. It is a slow process and takes time. Gaining 1 or 2 pounds of muscle a month is a realistic goal. When an athlete gains weight very rapidly (20 pounds in 3 months), most of the gain is probably fat or water retention.
4. Proper diet and rest are necessary for muscle growth. You must nourish your body with healthful foods that help muscle grow. And if you do not get enough rest, your muscles will not grow to potential.
5. Food supplements (protein powders, amino acids, etc.) can help if you do not eat a well-balanced diet of three meals a day. If you do eat well, supplements will be of little value because your body already receives all the nutrients it needs.

Anabolic Steroids

Recently you may have heard a lot about athletes who used anabolic steroids to get bigger and stronger. Many athletes who have admitted taking steroids have said it was not worth it. Not only is steroid use unethical and illegal, it can also cause unhealthy side effects: possible liver and kidney damage, increased risk of cardiovascular disease, psychological dependency on the drug, to name a few.

Because of this, I strongly suggest athletes stay away from steroids. By following a good strength program and eating a well-balanced diet, you will make great strength gains without using steroids.

CHAPTER 2

Strength-Training Guidelines

Before you start training, read every chapter of this book and familiarize yourself with the program. Study the exercise directions, the photographs, and the charts. Try to picture the whole year of training and see how each part relates to the others.

It's best if you have the book in hand by early January so you can follow the entire training routine as it leads up to the new football season. If you get the book at another time, begin with the next training cycle. For example, if you get the book in March and the next cycle starts in April, begin training in April. *Never start in the middle of a cycle.* Always start at the beginning of a cycle. That way, you'll get the most benefit and you'll reduce your chance of injury.

This book offers a suggested workout plan. Not everyone will be able to follow it in its entirety. Your ability to follow the plan will be affected by equipment availability, time, coaching supervision, previous injuries, level of expertise, and age. You may need to adjust the plan to suit your needs. Consult with your coach.

You should be able to perform each exercise. Refer to chapters 9 and 10 for instructions on how to do the exercises and photographs of models performing them. If you do not understand any part of this program, consult with your coach before continuing.

Remember to make each workout safe and productive. Safety guidelines are provided at the end of this chapter. The following explains several concepts you should understand before starting your workout program.

STRENGTH PROGRESS

Strength progress varies greatly among athletes. Probably the most important factor, besides genetic makeup, is how hard and how consistently you work. If you miss a few workouts here and there and do not give your best effort, you will not progress as well as someone who works harder and never misses a workout.

Here are some other factors that affect strength progress:

1. Novice athletes will make higher gains than experienced athletes. They have more room for improvement.
2. Bigger athletes with larger muscle mass will show higher gains than smaller athletes. For example, a lineman might add 20 pounds to his weight, whereas a receiver may add only 10 pounds.
3. Previous injuries can affect how well you perform and how much weight you can use in a particular exercise.
4. Other activities you do while you are strength training can affect your strength progress. If you are also doing a lot of running or are participating in another sport, your strength will not progress as much as if you were only strength training.

If you get no increases, or an actual decrease, in strength, consult with your coach and take a closer look at how these factors affect you.

As you know, each athlete has a different genetic potential for strength gains. Don't compare yourself with someone who is bigger or stronger. What should be important to you is that you are improving, which you can see as you progress to the next level of your program. Concentrate on reaching *your own* maximum potential.

THE PROGRAM CYCLE

A cycle is a systematic and organized training period. It has a specific starting and ending time. Each workout is planned with the exact exercises, sets, repetitions, and weight progression. During the year you will be involved with four cycles: two off-season cycles, a preseason cycle, and the season itself. In the first three cycles, you will try to accomplish specific goals so you can reach maximum strength before the season starts. In the last cycle, you will try to maintain that strength.

CHOOSING A LIFTING ROUTINE

There are two basic strength-training workout routines: the total-body routine and the split routine. In the total-body routine, you train three times per week, each time performing exercises that strengthen the whole body. In the split routine, you train four times per week with two workouts designed to strengthen the lower body (including the midsection and the lower back) and two workouts to strengthen the upper body.

This book presents both routines. You must choose one. Your schedule and weight-room limitations may influence your choice. For example, if you have time to train every day, then a split routine would work well for you. On the other hand, if the weight room is available only three times a week, you should use a total-body routine. Both routines are effective. Ask your coach which is best for you.

Weight Progression

The weight for each exercise in each workout is based on what you've done previously and on your ultimate goal. Be patient and consistent with your workouts. You'll need to work hard to reach your goals. The workouts are based on a systematic progression that will lead to strength gains.

All workouts in this book are based on percentages of the goals you set. It is important to follow the progression and percentages indicated. You should not lift heavily all the time, nor should you go easy all the time. When you use the percentage format, you know you are training at the right intensity based on your goals and abilities.

Sets and Repetitions

I have used a simple system for abbreviating the workouts in this book. For example, three sets of six repetitions is abbreviated 3×6. The first number always represents the number of sets, and the second number represents the number of repetitions.

A *set* is the completion of one or more repetitions performed consecutively without resting. If the workout shows 1×10, 1×8, 1×5, 1×3, 1×2, you will do a total of five sets in that exercise. *Repetitions* (often abbreviated as *reps*) are the number of times you do an exercise without resting during one set. For example, 1×10 means one set of 10 repetitions with the same weight.

Down Sets. *Down sets* are done after the heaviest set has been completed. They aid muscle growth. First you do a good progression leading up to the heavy weights, which will result in strength gains. Then, doing a few down sets builds additional muscle mass for further strength gains.

Core Versus Auxiliary Exercises

Core exercises (e.g., bench press, back squat, power clean) work many muscles simultaneously. Auxiliary exercises (e.g., bicep curls, leg curls) work one or a few muscles. A well-balanced program includes a combination of core and auxiliary exercises.

The muscles trained in each exercise are shown in Tables 2.1 and 2.2. Table 2.1 indicates the muscles that are worked in the core exercises, and Table 2.2 shows the muscles worked in the auxiliary exercises. Figure 2.1 illustrates these muscles.

Free Weights Versus Machines

To achieve optimal strength for football, you should train with barbells, dumbbells, and machines. Most exercises shown in this book use barbells because barbells are more common in today's weight rooms. Some of these exercises also can be performed with machines.

In many instances barbells are better for developing maximum strength and power. For example,

Table 2.1
Muscles Worked in Core Exercises

Exercise	Muscles worked
Bench press	Shoulders, chest, triceps
Incline press	Shoulders, triceps, upper chest, upper back
Behind-the-neck press	Shoulders, triceps, upper back
Back squat	Hips, hamstrings, quadriceps, groin, lower back
Leg press	Hips, quadriceps, hamstrings, groin
Dead lift	Hamstrings, quadriceps, groin, hips, lower back
Walking lunge	Groin, hips, hamstrings, quadriceps, ankles
Power clean, high pull	Legs, hips, calves, lower back, upper back, shoulders, ankles.

Table 2.2
Muscles Worked in Auxiliary Exercises

Exercise	Muscles worked
Neck—manual resistance	Neck flexors and extensors
Neck—variable resistance machines	Neck flexors and extensors
Alternate incline dumbbell presses	Shoulders (deltoids), triceps, upper chest
Dumbbell flys	Chest
Bicep curls	Biceps, forearms
Tricep extensions	Triceps
Dips	Shoulders, triceps
Wrist curls	Wrists, forearms
Bent-over rows	Latissimus dorsi, trapezius, rhomboids
Shoulder shrugs	Trapezius
Back raises	Spinal erectors (lower back)
Sit-up crunch	Abdominals
Oblique twists	Abdominals, obliques
Leg extensions	Quadriceps
Leg curls	Hamstrings
Standing heel raises	Ankles, calves

when you use a barbell you are in complete control of the weight, whereas when you use a machine, the machine helps support and stabilize the weight. Using a barbell provides more muscle work and more training for stabilizing muscles and tendons.

For other exercises, machines are better. For example, leg-curl machines are good for strengthening the hamstrings, and neck machines are good for strengthening the neck.

No apparatus or method is 100% injury-free. No matter what apparatus you use, you should use the proper technique and the proper amount of weight to prevent injuries.

SAFETY GUIDELINES

You will be successful at building strength only if you thoroughly understand the program and follow it. Strength training is not play; it is serious work. But it can be enjoyable when done correctly. Even under the best instruction and supervision, injuries can happen. To minimize your chance of injury, follow your coach's instructions and the following guidelines:

1. Get a physical evaluation by your doctor before starting any training program.

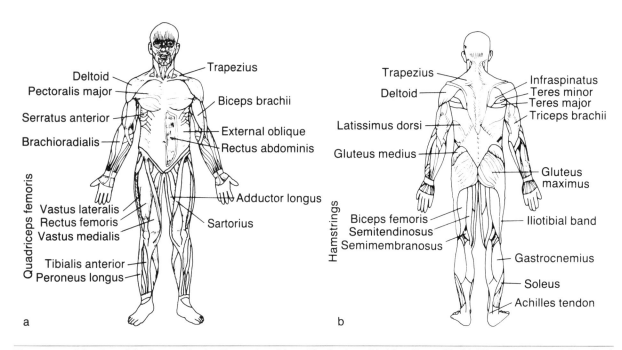

Figure 2.1 Muscles of the human body. Front view (a) and back view (b). *Note.* From *Health/Fitness Instructor's Handbook* (pp. 40-41) by E.T. Howley and B.D. Franks, 1986, Champaign, IL: Human Kinetics. Copyright 1986 by E.T. Howley and B.D. Franks. Adapted by permission.

2. Train only in the presence of a qualified coach. Do not train alone.
3. Consult with your coach before you begin, and continue to consult with him throughout the program. If you have any questions, ask him.
4. Train with partners so they can spot for you. Proper spotting is important. Spotters are there to assist in case you have difficulty.
5. Good technique is more important than the amount of weight you use, so always lift correctly. As time passes, the weight will increase.
6. If you have previous injuries, you will probably have to modify the program to accommodate your injured areas. Consult with your coach and your trainer or doctor.

CHAPTER 3

Designing Your Own Program

Before you start the program, assess your present strength level for each exercise.

DETERMINING YOUR STRENGTH LEVEL

If you have been training recently, determining your strength level is simple. Take your best effort for each exercise from your most recent workout or test. This is your present personal best. For example, if your recent best in the bench press is 240 pounds, your present personal best in the bench press is 240 pounds.

If you do not know your personal best in a particular exercise, get a calculated personal best by using the chart in Appendix D. For example, suppose your recent best in the incline press is 200 pounds for five reps. On the personal best conversion chart (see Table 3.1) look to column 5 (five reps), go down this column to the number 200, and follow across to column 1. Column 1 shows 220; this is your calculated personal best.

If you have never strength-trained or performed a particular exercise before, you need a starting point. Study the procedures for each exercise (see chapters 9 and 10) and practice with a coach and

a spotter, or spotters, until you are comfortable performing the exercise. Do not try to determine your personal best until you fully understand how to do an exercise.

Under the guidance of your coach, determine your strength level. Do not try to outdo yourself in this finding phase. Just get a general idea of your present strength in each exercise. Your age, size, and genetic potential determine your starting level. A 16-year-old weighing 180 pounds will probably start at a higher level than a 14-year-old who weighs 140 pounds.

Core Exercises

To determine your strength level for a particular exercise, refer to the following steps:

1. Do 10 repetitions of the exercise with just the bar. Rest for 2 minutes.
2. Add 10 pounds on each side and do 10 more repetitions. Rest for 2 minutes.
3. Add another 10 pounds on each side and do 10 more repetitions. Rest for 2 minutes.
4. Continue this process until you cannot do 10 full repetitions.
5. The last weight at which you can complete 10 repetitions becomes your strength level. Using this weight and the number of reps

Table 3.1
Sample Personal Best Conversion Chart

				Number of repetitions					
10	9	8	7	6	5	4	3	2	1
160	170	175	180	185	190	195	200	205	210
170	180	185	190	195	200	205	210	215	220
175	185	190	195	200	205	210	215	220	230

you completed (10), find your calculated single rep max using Appendix D.

6. Continue the same process for each core exercise.

7. Do not do more than three exercises per day. If you need to find your strength level in six exercises, do three on one day, the other three on the next. Spread the exercises out to be sure you get enough rest.

8. The 45-lb Olympic bar may be too heavy for you. If it is, use a standard bar, which weighs only 20 pounds, until you are strong enough to use the Olympic bar.

Auxiliary Exercises

To find your strength level for each auxiliary exercise, follow the same procedure. Begin with very light weights (5 to 10 pounds) and do 10 reps. Add a total of 5 pounds (2.5 pounds on each side) and do another 10 reps. Continue to increase the weight by these increments until you cannot complete 10 reps with the weight. Always rest 2 min between sets. The last weight you can perform for 10 reps becomes your new personal best. You do not have to convert your strength level for an auxiliary exercise to a calculated personal best. Use the auxiliary exercise weight progression chart in Appendix C to get the proper progression. (See chapter 4 for directions on how to use this chart.)

SETTING GOALS

Now that you have assessed your present strength level, set goals to be achieved by the end of each training cycle. Set goals for one cycle at a time. At the end of one cycle, set goals for the next. For the first three training cycles, you will set goals to improve strength. Your goal for the in-season will be to maintain the strength you have gained.

Remember, strength progress will vary greatly from one person to the next. If you are in your 1st or 2nd year of strength training, you will achieve considerable strength gains from one cycle to the next. You are still a novice in strength training, and your body is getting used to the weight and the technique. You have more room for improvement.

If you are in the intermediate level of strength training (if you have been lifting for 3 or 4 years), your progress will be slower than in your 1st 2 years. You have passed the learning stage and are closer to your strength potential. At this level, gains require more work.

Be realistic when setting goals. The goals should be challenging but attainable. In your core upper body exercises, set goals 10 to 15 pounds more than your present best. For lower body exercises, goals should be 20 to 30 pounds more than present best. For the power clean and the high pull, set your goals at 10 to 15 pounds more.

For example, if your present personal best in the bench press is 220 pounds, you might set a goal of 230 pounds for your next cycle. If your cycle goes well and you do 235 pounds at the end of the cycle, great. You surpassed your goal. For your next cycle, your goal might be 250 pounds (new personal best of 235 pounds plus 15 pounds).

You do not have to set goals for the auxiliary exercises. These exercises supplement the core exercises and help develop total body strength. You will want to increase the weights for the auxiliary exercises as you get stronger, but the increases should be small. Follow the directions in chapter 4.

Starting Your Program

This program for developing total body strength emphasizes the bench press, back squat, and power clean. These three exercises are the most important for developing football strength.

TRAINING CYCLES

Your training year is divided into four cycles: off-season I, off-season II, preseason, and in-season (see Table 4.1).

Table 4.1
Duration of Each Training Period

Training periods	Duration
Cycle 1 Off-season I	January-March
Cycle 2 Off-season II	March-June
Cycle 3 Preseason	June-August
Cycle 4 In-season	August-November

Note. Periods may vary from one program to another.

The goal of each training cycle is to reach a higher personal best (*max*) by the end of the cycle. To achieve a strong max, you need to build a solid base. The longer the cycle, the better your chance to improve your max. For this reason, each cycle begins with several sets and reps using moderate weights and progresses week by week, reducing the number of reps and increasing the weights.

For optimal gains you should not lift heavily in each exercise every day. In this program most core exercises are done at different intensities (percentages) throughout the week. Spreading the work load throughout the week and allowing your muscles to rest should lead to better results.

All intensities for the core exercises are based on percentages of the goals you set for yourself. This way, you get the most out of each workout. The percentages will guide you to work at *your own pace*. Everyone differs in strength, so just using general weights will not do. By setting personal goals and using the percentages given, you will have a program that is just for you.

Chapters 5 through 8 provide forms for you to fill out to record your personal training log. Your training log will give you the exercises to be done, the number of sets and reps, and the intensity for each exercise on each training day. You need only to fill in the blanks using the directions given in the section "Recording Your Workout" later in this chapter.

At the end of each training cycle, you will test to see if you have met the goals you set at the beginning of the cycle. Testing, a vital part of this program, is explained later in this chapter.

Between cycles you will have 1 to 4 weeks of no structured training. This phase, called *active rest*, is important to training. During this time you should stay active by lifting at a light intensity but do not follow a structured program. You may even find that for you complete rest is necessary. What is most important is that you are fresh and ready to work hard when you start a new training cycle. Use school closings, holidays, or vacations as your active rest periods. Consult with your coach about when to start and end each cycle.

RECORDING YOUR WORKOUT

It is easy to complete each workout plan by filling in the blanks in your daily log. Just use the following guidelines:

1. Choose one of the two lifting routines.
2. Write the date on each workout plan.
3. Fill in the blanks on a daily or weekly basis. Do not get too far ahead in filling the blanks, for you may need to modify your game plan.
4. Use the charts in Appendixes B and C to get the exact weight for each exercise and each set. Enter those numbers in the spaces provided.
5. Room is left at the bottom of each day's log for you or your coach to add other exercises. These can be exercises to strengthen a previous injury or to correct a muscular imbalance, or you might include an exercise specific to your position or one for an area that you simply want to do more work on.
6. After you complete the sets and reps for each exercise, check them off, showing you have done them in full without missing anything. Then you are ready to do the increased weight in the next workout.
7. If you cannot complete all the sets or reps at the prescribed weight, do not panic. Refer to the section "What if the Weights Are Too Heavy?" later in this chapter.
8. If you can do all the sets and reps at the prescribed weight and the workout is too easy, see the section "What If the Weights Are Too Light?" in this chapter.

Recording the Core Exercises

At the start of each cycle, you should have recorded your personal best (usually done in the previous cycle) for each exercise along with your goal for the present cycle. *You will use your goals to set the percentages for each workout.* (For instructions on how to set your goals, see chapter 3.) To illustrate how this is done, we'll use the following example:

Exercise	Personal Best	New Personal Goal
Bench press	285	300
Back squat	375	400
Power clean	240	250

In this example, your personal best in the bench press is 285 pounds and your goal is 300 pounds. All bench workouts for this cycle will be based on the 300-lb goal.

Look at your daily workout to see what exercises are to be done, the sets and reps, and, most importantly, at what percentages of your goal. A day's suggested workout might include three core exercises, using the following sets, reps, and intensities:

Bench press	_____	× 8
	_____	× 5
	_____	× 5
	_____	× 5
	_____	× 5 (75%)
Back squat	_____	× 8
	_____	× 5
	_____	× 5
	_____	× 3
	_____	× 3 (80%)
Power clean	_____	× 8
	_____	× 5
	_____	× 5
	_____	× 3
	_____	× 3
	_____	× 1 (95%)

The first step is to record the heaviest weight. Look in Appendix A to find the heaviest set with the pounds shown at that particular percentage. Remember, the percentage shown is for the *last heavy set.* For example, if your bench-press goal is 300 pounds, 75% of 300 is 225, so your last set of five reps should be done at 225 pounds. For a squat goal of 400 pounds, the last set of three reps should be done at 320 pounds (80% of 400). For a power-clean goal of 250 pounds, the last set of one rep should be done at 240 pounds (95% of 250).

Bench press   _____ × 8
     _____ × 5
     _____ × 5
     _____ × 5
     __225__ × 5 (75%)

Back squat   _____ × 8
     _____ × 5
     _____ × 5
     _____ × 3
     _____ × 3
     __320__ × 3 (80%)

Power clean   _____ × 8
     _____ × 5
     _____ × 5
     _____ × 3
     _____ × 3
     __240__ × 1 (95%)

Once you have recorded the heavy set for each core exercise, use Appendix B to fill in the sets leading up to the heaviest weight. These sets are usually referred to as *warm-up sets*.

Let's look at the bench press. The heavy set is to be done with 225 pounds. For this exercise you will do five sets. Go down the column in Table 4.2 labeled Set 5 to 225. From left to right, the numbers are 135, 155, 185, 205, 225.

Now record these numbers for each set:

Bench press   __135__ × 8
     __155__ × 5
     __185__ × 5
     __205__ × 5
     __225__ × 5 (75%)

By using the two charts, you have completed your bench workout plan with a specific weight for each set.

For the back squat, follow the same procedure. You will do six sets, so find 320 in the *sixth column* of Table 4.3 and fill in the remaining sets from the chart.

Record the numbers as shown below:

Back squat   __135__ × 8
     __185__ × 5
     __225__ × 5
     __280__ × 3
     __300__ × 3
     __320__ × 3 (80%)

Here again, your squat workout plan is complete with a specific weight for each set.

The power clean is to be performed for six sets with the last set at 240 pounds. Go down the sixth

Table 4.2
Sample Weight Progression Chart for the Bench Press

Set 1	Set 2	Set 3	Set 4	Set 5	Set 6
135	155	185	205	220	240
135	155	185	205	225	245
135	155	185	210	230	250

Table 4.3
Sample Weight Progression Chart for the Back Squat

Set 1	Set 2	Set 3	Set 4	Set 5	Set 6
135	185	225	275	295	315
135	185	225	280	300	320
135	185	245	285	305	325

column (Set 6) in Table 4.4 to 240. From left to right, the numbers are 135, 155, 185, 205, 220, 240. Each number represents the weight for its corresponding set.

Record those numbers for each set as shown below:

Power clean   135 × 8
                 155 × 5
                 185 × 5
                 205 × 3
                 220 × 3
                 240 × 1 (95%)

Now you have completed a day's workout plan for these three exercises.

Recording the Down Sets

All down sets are based on your heaviest set. If after you have completed the heaviest set, you are supposed to do two down sets, subtract the amount indicated on the workout form from your heaviest set.

Bench press   135 × 8
                 155 × 5
                 185 × 5
                 205 × 5
                 225 × 5 (75%)
                 205 × 8 (− 20)
                 205 × 8 (− 20)

The heavy set was done with 225 pounds for five repetitions; therefore, the two down sets are done using 205 pounds (225 − 20 = 205).

Recording the Auxiliary Exercises

Follow these steps to record your weights for the auxiliary exercises. Use the auxiliary exercise weight progression chart in Appendix C.

You'll do the auxiliary exercises at the end of the workout, so you do not need to do many warm-ups for them. As the chart shows, the weights of the three sets are relatively close, progressing for each set. The last set should be as heavy as you can handle for the number of repetitions prescribed.

Refer to last week's workout. If you completed all sets and reps for each auxiliary exercise, you should be able to use a heavier weight.

Bicep curls

    Last week   This week
    30 × 8   35 × 8
    40 × 8   45 × 8
    45 × 8   50 × 8

In this example, last week's sets were done at 30 pounds, 40 pounds, and 45 pounds and were completed as prescribed. This week you can go to the next line on the progression chart and record those numbers in the current log (see Table 4.5).

If not all the sets or reps were completed in the previous workout, stay with the same progression this week until you can complete them. For example, if in the last set of 45-lb bicep curls, you could do only six reps, this week you should stay with the same progression until you can do all of the reps in the last set. Then, progress in weight in the next workout.

If you are only doing two sets for a particular exercise, use the first two column numbers from the chart.

TESTING

Testing will show you, your coach, and your peers the strength progress you have made during a cycle. Because testing takes time away from training, it should not be done too often. Test only at the end of each cycle, and test only the bench

Table 4.4
Sample Weight Progression Chart for the Power Clean

Set 1	Set 2	Set 3	Set 4	Set 5	Set 6
135	155	185	200	215	235
135	155	185	205	220	240
135	155	185	205	225	245

Table 4.5
Sample Weight Progression Chart for Auxiliary Exercises

Set 1	Set 2	Set 3	
25	30	35	
30	35	40	
30	40	45	previous week
35	**45**	**50**	this week
40	50	55	
40	50	60	

press, back squat, and power clean. The test results are used to set new goals for the next cycle.

Your ultimate goal is to reach your best strength level right before the season starts, when it is most needed. During the season you will try to maintain that level. Some of you may even gain more strength, especially in the upper body.

Testing should be done early in the week when you are fresh from a weekend of rest. If you are really pressed for time, you may test all three exercises on the same day, but you will not get the best results. If you test the power clean on one day, take a day off, then test the bench press and the back squat on the third day; you will get much better, truer results.

Testing Methods

There are two methods of testing; both of which are effective:

1. *Single max* is the most common way of testing. In single max testing, after doing several warm-up sets, you lift as much as you can for one repetition.
2. In *rep max* testing, after doing the warm-up sets, you lift about 85% of your personal goal and do as many reps as you can. If you can do five reps at this percentage, you have reached your goal. If you can do only three or four, the goal has not been reached. If you can do more than five, you have surpassed your goal. Use Appendix D to see what your new max is.

Because you will test only three of your core exercises, you will need to use the personal best conversion chart in Appendix D to find your calculated personal best for the other core exercises. Then use the calculated personal best as a base for your next cycle.

Using the Personal Best Conversion Chart

This chart is a good guideline of what your single attempt would be, based on the number of repetitions you did at a particular weight. The numbers at the top of the chart are the number of repetitions completed. Under your number of repetitions find the amount of weight you used. Then look across to the last column on the right. That number is your calculated personal best.

Suppose you did 220 pounds for five repetitions. Look at Column 5 in Table 4.6 and follow down to 220. The number in the far right column is 250, so 250 pounds is your calculated personal best.

MODIFYING YOUR WORKOUT

Even with the best laid plans, you may run into situations where you need to modify your strength-training program: The workout may be too difficult or too easy for you to benefit from; your schedule may be interrupted, causing you to miss training days; or an injury may slow your progress. This section addresses these problems and offers possible ways to resolve them.

What If the Weights Are Too Heavy?

At some time you may find that you cannot keep up with the workout. You may be falling behind in one or more exercises. This can happen to anyone, even the most experienced lifter who trains diligently.

First, let's define *falling behind*. If one day you were supposed to do five reps in the last set of a

Table 4.6
Sample Personal Best Conversion Chart

10	9	8	7	6	5	4	3	2	1
185	195	200	205	210	215	220	225	230	240
190	200	205	210	215	220	230	235	240	250
200	210	215	220	225	230	240	245	250	260

heavy weight but could just do four, that is not falling behind. If this happens, just keep on going. It is probably just a daily low. But if in two or three consecutive workouts of the same exercise you cannot complete all the sets and reps, you are falling behind. For example, for the last set of the bench press you were supposed to do five heavy reps with 250 pounds but did only four reps. The following week you were supposed to do five reps at 260 pounds in the last set but did only three. This is falling behind because now there is a pattern.

When this happens, you must *drop* your goals by 5 to 10 pounds. If your goal in the bench press was 300 pounds, drop it to 290 pounds and base future workouts on this new goal. The week-by-week percentage increases and the sets and reps scheduled should not change. *Change only your goals.*

There are many reasons for falling behind. Usually is is because goals were set too high. Whatever the reason, you must adapt to the change so that future workouts will be productive (you'll do all sets and reps) without taking the chance of burnout and injury. This will help you get to the testing date fresh and able to perform at your best.

What If the Weights Are Too Light?

You may find that the workout for an exercise is too easy. You can do all the heavy sets and reps with no problem, and you think you could do more. If this happens for two consecutive workouts with the same exercise, you may have set your goals too low.

To remedy the situation, *add* 5 to 10 pounds to your goal. For example, your workouts for the back squat were based on a goal of 400 lb. Add 10 pounds to your goal and base all future workout numbers on 410 pounds. Here again, the sets, reps, and weekly percentage increase should stay the same. *Change only your goal.*

What If I Miss Training Days?

When you participate in a competitive sport like football, you cannot afford to miss training days. As my coach told me when I was an aspiring Olympian, "If you do not train today, someone somewhere is training and is gaining an edge on you." Do everything in your power to avoid missing training days and to be consistent in your workouts. Unfortunately, circumstances beyond your control (sickness, injuries, family vacations, etc.) will force you to miss training days. When this happens, adjust your training schedule accordingly. For example, during an 8-week training cycle, you go on a vacation with your family for 2 weeks. You miss Weeks 4 and 5 of your cycle. When you return, you cannot just jump into the workout for Week 6 and expect to do well. You need to backtrack somewhat. Table 4.7 shows you what percentage to resume your workout at, based on where you would have been if your workout had not been interrupted.

Because you missed workouts, you will not be able to go as heavily as planned in the last 2 weeks. Consult with your coach to make the proper adjustments.

What If I Am Injured?

Football is a physical sport with a lot of contact. By its nature it has a higher incidence of injury than most other sports. Any injury can slow your strength progress. Even an injury that occurred during the season might affect you during the following off-season of strength training.

If you get injured, you will have to modify your training plan. For example, if you have a knee injury, you might not be able to do back squats but exercises not related to the knee (e.g., bench press, incline press) can progress normally. As for the lower body, follow the advice of your doctor, trainer, and coach. When you have fully recovered, you should be able to resume training in that area and to follow the guidelines in this book.

Table 4.7
Sample Training Schedule Modification

Week	Planned	Actual
Week 1	78%	78%
Week 2	82%	82%
Week 3	85%	85%
Week 4	87%	Vacation
Week 5	90%	Vacation
Week 6	94%	87%
Week 7	97%	90%
Week 8	Testing	Testing

THE YEARLY
WORKOUT PLAN

CHAPTER 5

Off-Season I Workout

This first cycle should start in January when school is back in session and end in March close to spring break or at the start of spring ball. This sample workout is for 9 weeks of training plus 1 week for testing. If your school calendar allows only 7 weeks for training, delete Weeks 2 and 4 from the program. If you have only 8 weeks for training, delete Week 2. Be sure to consult with your coach when modifying the workout plan.

This is the time of the year to make big gains in strength. Most of your time and energy should be devoted to strength training. If you participate in a winter sport (basketball, wrestling, etc.), you will have to modify the program. Consult with your coach and find a happy medium so you can participate in your sport and continue your physical development.

WORKOUT GOALS

Enter your personal best for the exercises that were tested or the calculated personal best for all of the exercises. Remember, the number should represent one *single* repetition personal best.

Now set the goals you want to achieve by the end of the cycle. Be reasonable in setting goals. Make them challenging but not unobtainable. Your goals will be used to calculate how heavily you will train during this cycle.

As for your auxiliary exercises, use moderate weights at first (based on what you have done in the past) and progress when you can, following the direction in chapter 4.

Exercise	Personal Best	New Personal Goal
Bench press	_____	_____
Back squat	_____	_____
Power clean	_____	_____
Incline press	_____	_____
Behind-the-neck press	_____	_____
High pull	_____	_____

WORKOUT CHARTS

Pages 22-35 contain the workout charts you'll follow for your first off-season workout. You may choose either the split routine (MTuThF) or the total-body routine (MWF).

Off-Season I
Split Routine
Mondays

Date:

Exercise	Week 1	Week 2	Week 3	Week 4	Week 5
Incline press	___× 10	___× 10	___× 10	___× 10	___× 10
	___× 10	___× 10	___× 8	___× 8	___× 8
	___× 10	___× 10	___× 8	___× 8	___× 8
	___× 10 (50%)	___× 10 (55%)	___× 8	___× 8	___× 8
			___× 8 (60%)	___× 8 (62%)	___× 8 (65%)
Bench press	___× 10	___× 10	___× 10	___× 10	___× 10
	___× 10	___× 10	___× 8	___× 8	___× 8
	___× 10	___× 10	___× 8	___× 8	___× 8
	___× 10 (50%)	___× 10 (60%)	___× 8	___× 8	___× 8
			___× 8 (62%)	___× 8 (65%)	___× 8 (65%)
Shoulder shrugs	___× 10	___× 10	___× 10	___× 10	___× 10
	___× 10	___× 10	___× 10	___× 8	___× 8
	___× 10	___× 10	___× 10	___× 8	___× 8
Bicep curls	___× 10	___× 10	___× 10	___× 10	___× 10
	___× 10	___× 10	___× 10	___× 8	___× 8
	___× 10	___× 10	___× 10	___× 8	___× 8
Dumbbell flys	___× 10	___× 10	___× 10	___× 10	___× 10
	___× 10	___× 10	___× 10	___× 8	___× 8
	___× 10	___× 10	___× 10	___× 8	___× 8
Dips	___×___	___×___	___×___	___×___	___×___
	___×___	___×___	___×___	___×___	___×___
	___×___	___×___	___×___	___×___	___×___

Additional exercises:

Off-Season I
Split Routine
Mondays (continued)

Date:	_____	_____	_____	_____	_____
Exercise	**Week 6**	**Week 7**	**Week 8**	**Week 9**	**Week 10 Test week**
Incline press	___× 10	___× 10	___× 10	___× 8	
	___× 8	___× 8	___× 8	___× 6	
	___× 6	___× 6	___× 6	___× 5	
	___× 6	___× 6	___× 5	___× 3 (80%)	
	___× 6 (67%)	___× 6 (70%)	___× 5 (75%)		
Bench press	___× 10	___× 10	___× 10	___× 8	
	___× 8	___× 8	___× 8	___× 6	
	___× 6	___× 6	___× 6	___× 5	
	___× 6	___× 6	___× 5	___× 3 (80%)	
	___× 6 (67%)	___× 6 (70%)	___× 5 (75%)		
Shoulder shrugs	___× 10	___× 10	___× 10	___× 10	
	___× 8	___× 8	___× 8	___× 8	
	___× 8	___× 6	___× 6	___× 6	
Bicep curls	___× 10	___× 10	___× 10	___× 10	
	___× 8	___× 8	___× 8	___× 8	
	___× 8	___× 6	___× 6	___× 6	
Dumbbell flys	___× 10	___× 10	___× 10	___× 10	
	___× 8	___× 8	___× 8	___× 8	
	___× 8	___× 6	___× 6	___× 6	
Dips	___×___	___×___	___×___	___×___	
	___×___	___×___	___×___	___×___	
	___×___	___×___	___×___	___×___	

Additional exercises:

Off-Season I
Split Routine
Tuesdays

Date:	_____	_____	_____	_____	_____
Exercise	**Week 1**	**Week 2**	**Week 3**	**Week 4**	**Week 5**
Back squat	___× 10	___× 10	___× 10	___× 10	___× 10
	___× 10	___× 10	___× 8	___× 8	___× 8
	___× 10	___× 10	___× 8	___× 6	___× 6
	___× 10 (50%)	___× 10 (60%)	___× 8	___× 4	___× 4
			___× 8 (70%)	___× 6 (72%)	___× 6 (75%)
				___× 8 (− 40)	___× 8 (− 40)
				___× 8 (− 40)	___× 8 (− 40)
High pull	___× 8	___× 8	___× 5	___× 5	___× 5
	___× 5	___× 5	___× 5	___× 5	___× 5
	___× 5	___× 5	___× 5	___× 5	___× 5
	___× 5 (50%)	___× 5 (55%)	___× 5	___× 4	___× 4
			___× 5 (60%)	___× 4 (62%)	___× 4 (67%)
Walking lunge (each leg)	___× 6	___× 6	___× 6	___× 5	___× 5
	___× 6	___× 6	___× 6	___× 5	___× 5
	___× 6	___× 6	___× 6	___× 5	___× 5
Back raises	___× 10	___× 10	___× 10	___× 10	___× 10
	___× 10	___× 10	___× 10	___× 8	___× 8
	___× 10	___× 10	___× 10	___× 8	___× 8
Standing heel raises	___× 10	___× 10	___× 10	___× 10	___× 10
	___× 10	___× 10	___× 10	___× 8	___× 8
	___× 10	___× 10	___× 10	___× 8	___× 8
Neck resistance	___× 10	___× 10	___× 10	___× 10	___× 10
	___× 10	___× 10	___× 10	___× 8	___× 8
Sit-up crunch	___×___	___×___	___×___	___×___	___×___
	___×___	___×___	___×___	___×___	___×___
	___×___	___×___	___×___	___×___	___×___

Additional exercises:

Off-Season I
Split Routine
Tuesdays (continued)

Exercise	Week 6	Week 7	Week 8	Week 9	Week 10 Test week
Date:	_____	_____	_____	_____	_____
Back squat	____× 10	____× 10	____× 10	____× 10	
	____× 8	____× 8	____× 8	____× 8	
	____× 5	____× 5	____× 5	____× 5	
	____× 3	____× 3	____× 2	____× 2	
	____× 5 (77%)	____× 5 (80%)	____× 3 (85%)	____× 3 (90%)	
	____× 8 (− 40)	____× 8 (− 40)	____× 6 (− 40)		
	____× 8 (− 40)	____× 8 (− 40)	____× 6 (− 40)		
High pull	____× 5	____× 5	____× 5	____× 5	
	____× 5	____× 5	____× 5	____× 5	
	____× 4	____× 4	____× 3	____× 3	
	____× 3	____× 3	____× 3	____× 3	
	____× 3 (67%)	____× 3 (70%)	____× 2 (75%)	____× 2 (80%)	
Walking lunge (each leg)	____× 5	____× 4	____× 4	____× 4	
	____× 5	____× 4	____× 4	____× 4	
	____× 5	____× 4	____× 4	____× 4	
Back raises	____× 10	____× 10	____× 10	____× 10	
	____× 8	____× 8	____× 8	____× 8	
	____× 8	____× 6	____× 6	____× 6	
Standing heel raises	____× 10	____× 10	____× 10	____× 10	
	____× 8	____× 8	____× 8	____× 8	
	____× 8	____× 6	____× 6	____× 6	
Neck resistance	____× 10	____× 8	____× 8	____× 8	
	____× 8	____× 6	____× 6	____× 6	
Sit-up crunch	____×____	____×____	____×____	____×____	
	____×____	____×____	____×____	____×____	
	____×____	____×____	____×____	____×____	

Additional exercises:

25

Off-Season I
Split Routine
Thursdays

Exercise	Week 1	Week 2	Week 3	Week 4	Week 5
Date:	_____	_____	_____	_____	_____
Bench press	___× 10	___× 10	___× 10	___× 10	___× 10
	___× 10	___× 10	___× 8	___× 8	___× 8
	___× 10	___× 10	___× 8	___× 6	___× 6
	___× 10 (55%)	___× 10 (65%)	___× 8	___× 4	___× 4
			___× 8 (70%)	___× 6 (72%)	___× 6 (75%)
				___× 8 (− 30)	___× 8 (− 30)
				___× 8 (− 30)	___× 8 (− 30)
Behind-the-neck press	___× 10	___× 10	___× 10	___× 10	___× 10
	___× 10	___× 10	___× 8	___× 8	___× 8
	___× 10 (55%)	___× 10 (55%)	___× 8	___× 8	___× 8
			___× 8 (60%)	___× 8 (62%)	___× 8 (65%)
Bent-over rows	___× 10	___× 10	___× 10	___× 10	___× 10
	___× 10	___× 10	___× 10	___× 8	___× 8
	___× 10	___× 10	___× 10	___× 8	___× 8
Alternate incline dumb-bell presses	___× 10	___× 10	___× 10	___× 10	___× 10
	___× 10	___× 10	___× 10	___× 8	___× 8
	___× 10	___× 10	___× 10	___× 8	___× 8
Bicep curls	___× 10	___× 10	___× 10	___× 10	___× 10
	___× 10	___× 10	___× 10	___× 8	___× 8
	___× 10	___× 10	___× 10	___× 8	___× 8
Wrist curls	___× 10	___× 10	___× 10	___× 10	___× 10
	___× 10	___× 10	___× 10	___× 8	___× 8

Additional exercises:

Off-Season I
Split Routine
Thursdays (continued)

Exercise	Week 6	Week 7	Week 8	Week 9	Week 10 Test week
Date:	_____	_____	_____	_____	_____
Bench press	___× 10	___× 10	___× 10	___× 10	
	___× 8	___× 8	___× 8	___× 8	
	___× 5	___× 5	___× 5	___× 5	
	___× 3	___× 3	___× 2	___× 2	
	___× 5 (78%)	___× 5 (80%)	___× 3 (85%)	___× 3 (90%)	
	___× 8 (− 30)	___× 8 (− 30)	___× 6 (− 30)		
	___× 8 (− 30)	___× 8 (− 30)	___× 6 (− 30)		
Behind-the-neck press	___× 10	___× 10	___× 10	___× 10	
	___× 8	___× 8	___× 8	___× 8	
	___× 6	___× 6	___× 6	___× 6	
	___× 6 (68%)	___× 6 (70%)	___× 5 (72%)	___× 5 (72%)	
Bent-over rows	___× 10	___× 10	___× 10		
	___× 8	___× 8	___× 8		
	___× 8	___× 6	___× 6		
Alternate incline dumb-bell presses	___× 10	___× 10	___× 10		
	___× 8	___× 8	___× 8		
	___× 8	___× 6	___× 6		
Bicep curls	___× 10	___× 10	___× 10		
	___× 8	___× 8	___× 8		
	___× 8	___× 6	___× 6		
Wrist curls	___× 10	___× 8	___× 8		
	___× 8	___× 6	___× 6		

Additional exercises:

Off-Season I
Split Routine
Fridays

Date:					
Exercise	**Week 1**	**Week 2**	**Week 3**	**Week 4**	**Week 5**
Power clean	___× 8	___× 8	___× 8	___× 5	___× 5
	___× 5	___× 5	___× 5	___× 5	___× 5
	___× 5	___× 5	___× 5	___× 5	___× 5
	___× 5 (60%)	___× 5 (65%)	___× 5	___× 4	___× 4
			___× 5 (68%)	___× 4 (72%)	___× 4 (75%)
Back squat	___× 10	___× 10	___× 10	___× 8	___× 10
	___× 10	___× 10	___× 8	___× 8	___× 8
	___× 10	___× 10	___× 8	___× 8	___× 8
	___× 10 (55%)	___× 10 (60%)	___× 8	___× 8	___× 8
			___× 8 (64%)	___× 8 (66%)	___× 8 (68%)
Leg curls	___× 10	___× 10	___× 10	___× 10	___× 10
	___× 10	___× 10	___× 10	___× 8	___× 8
	___× 10	___× 10	___× 10	___× 8	___× 8
Leg extensions	___× 10	___× 10	___× 10	___× 10	___× 10
	___× 10	___× 10	___× 10	___× 8	___× 8
	___× 10	___× 10	___× 10	___× 8	___× 8
Oblique twists	___× 10	___× 10	___× 10	___× 10	___× 10
	___× 10	___× 10	___× 10	___× 8	___× 8
	___× 10	___× 10	___× 10	___× 8	___× 8
Neck resistance	___× 10	___× 10	___× 10	___× 10	___× 10
	___× 10	___× 10	___× 10	___× 8	___× 8
Sit-up crunch	___×___	___×___	___×___	___×___	___×___
	___×___	___×___	___×___	___×___	___×___

Additional exercises:

Date:	_____	_____	_____	_____	_____
Exercise	**Week 6**	**Week 7**	**Week 8**	**Week 9**	**Week 10** **Test week**
Power clean	____× 5	____× 5	____× 5	____× 5	
	____× 5	____× 5	____× 5	____× 5	
	____× 4	____× 4	____× 3	____× 3	
	____× 3	____× 3	____× 3	____× 2 (90%)	
	____× 3 (80%)	____× 3 (82%)	____× 2 (85%)		
Back squat	____× 10	____× 10	____× 10	____× 8	
	____× 8	____× 8	____× 8	____× 6	
	____× 6	____× 6	____× 6	____× 5	
	____× 6	____× 6	____× 5	____× 3 (85%)	
	____× 6 (72%)	____× 6 (75%)	____× 5 (80%)		
Leg curls	____× 10	____× 10	____× 10		
	____× 8	____× 8	____× 8		
	____× 8	____× 6	____× 6		
Leg extensions	____× 10	____× 10	____× 10		
	____× 8	____× 8	____× 8		
	____× 8	____× 6	____× 6		
Oblique twists	____× 10	____× 10	____× 10		
	____× 8	____× 8	____× 8		
	____× 8	____× 6	____× 6		
Neck resistance	____× 10	____× 8	____× 8		
	____× 8	____× 6	____× 6		
Sit-up crunch	____×____	____×____	____×____		
	____×____	____×____	____×____		

Additional exercises:

Off-Season I
Total-Body Routine
Mondays

Date:	_____	_____	_____	_____	_____
Exercise	**Week 1**	**Week 2**	**Week 3**	**Week 4**	**Week 5**
Bench press	___ × 10	___ × 10	___ × 10	___ × 10	___ × 10
	___ × 10	___ × 10	___ × 8	___ × 8	___ × 8
	___ × 10	___ × 10	___ × 8	___ × 6	___ × 6
	___ × 10 (50%)	___ × 10 (60%)	___ × 8	___ × 4	___ × 4
			___ × 8 (68%)	___ × 6 (72%)	___ × 6 (77%)
				___ × 8 (− 30)	___ × 8 (− 30)
				___ × 8 (− 30)	___ × 8 (− 30)
Back squat	___ × 10	___ × 10	___ × 10	___ × 10	___ × 10
	___ × 10	___ × 10	___ × 8	___ × 8	___ × 8
	___ × 10	___ × 10	___ × 8	___ × 8	___ × 8
	___ × 10 (50%)	___ × 10 (60%)	___ × 8	___ × 8	___ × 8
			___ × 8 (65%)	___ × 8 (68%)	___ × 8 (70%)
Incline press	___ × 10	___ × 10	___ × 10	___ × 10	___ × 10
	___ × 10	___ × 10	___ × 8	___ × 8	___ × 8
	___ × 10 (50%)	___ × 10 (55%)	___ × 8	___ × 8	___ × 8
			___ × 8 (60%)	___ × 8 (62%)	___ × 8 (65%)
Bent-over rows	___ × 10	___ × 10	___ × 10	___ × 10	___ × 10
	___ × 10	___ × 10	___ × 10	___ × 8	___ × 8
	___ × 10	___ × 10	___ × 10	___ × 8	___ × 8
Leg curls	___ × 10	___ × 10	___ × 10	___ × 10	___ × 10
	___ × 10	___ × 10	___ × 10	___ × 8	___ × 8
	___ × 10	___ × 10	___ × 10	___ × 8	___ × 8
Bicep curls	___ × 10	___ × 10	___ × 10	___ × 10	___ × 10
	___ × 10	___ × 10	___ × 10	___ × 8	___ × 8
	___ × 10	___ × 10	___ × 10	___ × 8	___ × 8
Standing heel raises	___ × 10	___ × 10	___ × 10	___ × 10	___ × 10
	___ × 10	___ × 10	___ × 10	___ × 8	___ × 8
Neck resistance	___ × 10	___ × 10	___ × 10	___ × 10	___ × 10
	___ × 10	___ × 10	___ × 10	___ × 8	___ × 8
Sit-up crunch	___ × ___	___ × ___	___ × ___	___ × ___	___ × ___
	___ × ___	___ × ___	___ × ___	___ × ___	___ × ___
	___ × ___	___ × ___	___ × ___	___ × ___	___ × ___

Additional exercises:

Off-Season I
Total-Body Routine
Mondays (continued)

Exercise	Week 6	Week 7	Week 8	Week 9	Week 10 Test week
Date:	_____	_____	_____	_____	_____
Bench press	___ × 10	___ × 10	___ × 10	___ × 10	
	___ × 8	___ × 8	___ × 8	___ × 8	
	___ × 5	___ × 5	___ × 5	___ × 5	
	___ × 3	___ × 3	___ × 2	___ × 2	
	___ × 5 (77%)	___ × 5 (80%)	___ × 3 (85%)	___ × 3 (90%)	
	___ × 8 (− 30)	___ × 8 (− 30)	___ × 6 (− 30)		
	___ × 8 (− 30)	___ × 8 (− 30)	___ × 6 (− 30)		
Back squat	___ × 10	___ × 10	___ × 10	___ × 10	
	___ × 8	___ × 8	___ × 8	___ × 8	
	___ × 6	___ × 6	___ × 6	___ × 6	
	___ × 6	___ × 6	___ × 5	___ × 5	
	___ × 6 (75%)	___ × 6 (77%)	___ × 5 (80%)	___ × 5 (82%)	
Incline press	___ × 10	___ × 10	___ × 10	___ × 10	
	___ × 8	___ × 8	___ × 8	___ × 8	
	___ × 6	___ × 6	___ × 6	___ × 6	
	___ × 6 (68%)	___ × 6 (70%)	___ × 5 (72%)	___ × 5 (75%)	
Bent-over rows	___ × 10	___ × 10	___ × 10	___ × 10	
	___ × 8	___ × 8	___ × 8	___ × 8	
	___ × 8	___ × 6	___ × 6	___ × 6	
Leg curls	___ × 10	___ × 8	___ × 8	___ × 8	
	___ × 8	___ × 8	___ × 8	___ × 8	
	___ × 8	___ × 6	___ × 6	___ × 6	
Bicep curls	___ × 10	___ × 8	___ × 8	___ × 8	
	___ × 8	___ × 8	___ × 8	___ × 8	
	___ × 8	___ × 6	___ × 6	___ × 6	
Standing heel raises	___ × 10	___ × 8	___ × 8	___ × 8	
	___ × 8	___ × 6	___ × 6	___ × 6	
Neck resistance	___ × 10	___ × 8	___ × 8	___ × 8	
	___ × 8	___ × 6	___ × 6	___ × 6	
Sit-up crunch	___ × ___	___ × ___	___ × ___	___ × ___	
	___ × ___	___ × ___	___ × ___	___ × ___	
	___ × ___	___ × ___	___ × ___	___ × ___	

Additional exercises:

Off-Season I
Total-Body Routine
Wednesdays

Exercise	Week 1	Week 2	Week 3	Week 4	Week 5
Date:	_____	_____	_____	_____	_____
Power clean	___× 8	___× 8	___× 8	___× 5	___× 5
	___× 5	___× 5	___× 5	___× 5	___× 5
	___× 5	___× 5	___× 5	___× 5	___× 5
	___× 5 (60%)	___× 5 (65%)	___× 5	___× 4	___× 4
			___× 5 (68%)	___× 4 (72%)	___× 4 (75%)
Incline press	___× 10	___× 10	___× 10	___× 10	___× 10
	___× 10	___× 10	___× 8	___× 8	___× 8
	___× 10	___× 10	___× 8	___× 8	___× 8
	___× 10 (55%)	___× 10 (60%)	___× 8	___× 8	___× 8
			___× 8 (65%)	___× 8 (68%)	___× 8 (70%)
Walking lunge (each leg)	___× 5	___× 5	___× 5	___× 4	___× 4
	___× 5	___× 5	___× 5	___× 4	___× 4
	___× 5	___× 5	___× 5	___× 4	___× 4
Bent-over rows	___× 10	___× 10	___× 10	___× 10	___× 10
	___× 10	___× 10	___× 10	___× 8	___× 8
	___× 10	___× 10	___× 10	___× 8	___× 8
Tricep extensions	___× 10	___× 10	___× 10	___× 8	___× 8
	___× 10	___× 10	___× 10	___× 8	___× 8
	___× 10	___× 10	___× 10	___× 8	___× 8
Back raises	___× 10	___× 10	___× 10	___× 10	___× 10
	___× 10	___× 10	___× 10	___× 8	___× 8
Standing heel raises	___× 10	___× 10	___× 10	___× 10	___× 10
	___× 10	___× 10	___× 10	___× 8	___× 8
Neck resistance	___× 10	___× 10	___× 10	___× 10	___× 10
	___× 10	___× 10	___× 10	___× 8	___× 8

Additional exercises:

Off-Season I
Total-Body Routine
Wednesdays (continued)

Date:	_____	_____	_____	_____	_____
Exercise	**Week 6**	**Week 7**	**Week 8**	**Week 9**	**Week 10** **Test week**
Power clean	___× 5	___× 5	___× 5	___× 5	
	___× 5	___× 5	___× 5	___× 4	
	___× 4	___× 4	___× 3	___× 3	
	___× 3	___× 3	___× 3	___× 2 (90%)	
	___× 3 (80%)	___× 2 (82%)	___× 2 (85%)		
Incline press	___× 10	___× 10	___× 10	___× 10	
	___× 10	___× 10	___× 8	___× 8	
	___× 6	___× 6	___× 6	___× 6	
	___× 6	___× 6	___× 5	___× 5	
	___× 6 (72%)	___× 6 (75%)	___× 5 (78%)	___× 5 (80%)	
Walking lunge (each leg)	___× 4	___× 4	___× 4	___× 4	
	___× 4	___× 4	___× 4	___× 4	
	___× 4	___× 4	___× 4	___× 4	
Bent-over rows	___× 10	___× 10	___× 10	___× 10	
	___× 8	___× 8	___× 8	___× 8	
	___× 8	___× 6	___× 6	___× 6	
Tricep extensions	___× 10	___× 10	___× 10	___× 10	
	___× 8	___× 8	___× 8	___× 8	
	___× 8	___× 6	___× 6	___× 6	
Back raises	___× 10	___× 10	___× 10	___× 10	
	___× 8	___× 8	___× 8	___× 8	
Standing heel raises	___× 10	___× 10	___× 10	___× 10	
	___× 8	___× 8	___× 8	___× 8	
Neck resistance	___× 10	___× 8	___× 8	___× 8	
	___× 8	___× 6	___× 6	___× 6	

Additional exercises:

Off-Season I
Total-Body Routine
Fridays

Date:	_____	_____	_____	_____	_____
Exercise	**Week 1**	**Week 2**	**Week 3**	**Week 4**	**Week 5**
Back squat	___× 10	___× 10	___× 10	___× 10	___× 10
	___× 10	___× 10	___× 8	___× 8	___× 8
	___× 10	___× 10	___× 8	___× 6	___× 6
	___× 10 (55%)	___× 10 (62%)	___× 8	___× 4	___× 4
			___× 8 (70%)	___× 6 (72%)	___× 6 (75%)
				___× 8 (− 40)	___× 8 (− 40)
				___× 8 (− 40)	___× 8 (− 40)
Bench press	___× 10	___× 10	___× 10	___× 10	___× 10
	___× 10	___× 10	___× 8	___× 8	___× 8
	___× 10	___× 10	___× 8	___× 8	___× 8
	___× 10 (55%)	___× 10 (60%)	___× 8	___× 8	___× 8
			___× 8 (60%)	___× 8 (62%)	___× 8 (65%)
Behind-the-neck press	___× 10	___× 10	___× 10	___× 10	___× 10
	___× 10	___× 10	___× 8	___× 8	___× 8
	___× 10 (50%)	___× 10 (54%)	___× 8	___× 8	___× 8
			___× 8 (56%)	___× 8 (58%)	___× 8 (60%)
Bent-over rows	___× 10	___× 10	___× 10	___× 10	___× 10
	___× 10	___× 10	___× 10	___× 8	___× 8
	___× 10	___× 10	___× 10	___× 8	___× 8
Shoulder shrugs	___× 10	___× 10	___× 10	___× 10	___× 10
	___× 10	___× 10	___× 10	___× 8	___× 8
	___× 10	___× 10	___× 10	___× 8	___× 8
Bicep curls	___× 10	___× 10	___× 10	___× 10	___× 10
	___× 10	___× 10	___× 10	___× 8	___× 8
	___× 10	___× 10	___× 10	___× 8	___× 8
Leg curls	___× 10	___× 10	___× 10	___× 10	___× 10
	___× 10	___× 10	___× 10	___× 8	___× 8
Neck resistance	___× 10	___× 10	___× 10	___× 10	___× 10
	___× 10	___× 10	___× 10	___× 8	___× 8
Sit-up crunch	___×___	___×___	___×___	___×___	___×___
	___×___	___×___	___×___	___×___	___×___

Additional exercises:

Date:

Exercise	Week 6	Week 7	Week 8	Week 9	Week 10 Test week
Back squat	___× 10	___× 10	___× 10	___× 10	
	___× 8	___× 8	___× 8	___× 8	
	___× 5	___× 5	___× 5	___× 5	
	___× 3	___× 3	___× 2	___× 2	
	___× 5 (77%)	___× 5 (80%)	___× 3 (85%)	___× 3 (90%)	
	___× 8 (− 40)	___× 8 (− 40)	___× 6 (− 40)		
	___× 8 (− 40)	___× 8 (− 40)	___× 6 (− 40)		
Bench press	___× 10	___× 10	___× 10	___× 10	
	___× 8	___× 8	___× 8	___× 8	
	___× 6	___× 6	___× 6	___× 6	
	___× 6	___× 6	___× 5	___× 5	
	___× 6 (67%)	___× 6 (70%)	___× 5 (75%)	___× 5 (80%)	
Behind-the-neck press	___× 10	___× 10	___× 10	___× 10	
	___× 8	___× 8	___× 8	___× 8	
	___× 6	___× 6	___× 5	___× 5	
	___× 6 (62%)	___× 6 (65%)	___× 5 (68%)	___× 5 (70%)	
Bent-over rows	___× 10	___× 10	___× 10		
	___× 8	___× 8	___× 8		
	___× 8	___× 6	___× 6		
Shoulder shrugs	___× 10	___× 10	___× 10		
	___× 8	___× 8	___× 8		
	___× 8	___× 6	___× 6		
Bicep curls	___× 10	___× 10	___× 10		
	___× 8	___× 8	___× 8		
	___× 8	___× 6	___× 6		
Leg curls	___× 10	___× 8	___× 8		
	___× 8	___× 6	___× 6		
Neck resistance	___× 10	___× 8	___× 8		
	___× 8	___× 6	___× 6		
Sit-up crunch	___×___	___×___	___×___		
	___×___	___×___	___×___		

Additional exercises:

TEST WEEK

The 10th week of each routine is devoted to testing. Use the following guidelines and the chart provided while testing your progress.

1. Test in the presence of your coach.
2. Review the section on testing in chapter 4.
3. Choose between single max and rep max testing methods.
4. Record your goal weight.
5. Using the core exercise weight progression chart in Appendix B, fill in the weights for the warm-up sets leading up to your heavy set, just as you would do for a regular workout.
6. If during single max testing you reach your goal and think you can do more, try another single with a 5- to 10-lb increase.
7. For rep max testing do as many reps as you can with the final weight. Figure your calculated personal best by using the personal best conversion chart (Appendix D).
8. If you are lifting very heavy weights, you may need more warm-up sets.
9. For your other core exercises that you are not actually testing (e.g., incline press), take your last workout weight and use Appendix D to determine your calculated personal best.
10. Remember, you do not need to test auxiliary exercises.
11. If you have met your goals, great. If you've surpassed them, even better. If you did not reach your goals, reevaluate your goal-setting procedures.

SINGLE MAX TESTING

Power clean	Bench press	Back squat
_____ × 5	_____ × 8	_____ × 8
_____ × 3	_____ × 5	_____ × 5
_____ × 2	_____ × 3	_____ × 3
_____ × 1	_____ × 2	_____ × 2
_____ × 1 (goal)	_____ × 1	_____ × 1
	_____ × 1 (goal)	_____ × 1 (goal)

REP MAX TESTING

Power clean	Bench press	Back squat
_____ × 5	_____ × 8	_____ × 8
_____ × 3	_____ × 5	_____ × 5
_____ × 2	_____ × 3	_____ × 3
_____ × 3 (93% of goal)	_____ × 5 (85% of goal)	_____ × 5 (85% of goal)

CHAPTER 6

Off-Season II Workout

This second cycle should start in March after spring break or after the start of spring ball. It should end right before the end of the school year in early June.

This sample workout is for 9 weeks of training plus 1 week for testing. If your school calendar allows only 7 weeks for training, delete Weeks 2 and 4. If you have only 8 weeks for training, delete Week 2 from the program. Consult with your coach when modifying the workout plan.

You must continue to improve in strength during this cycle, as you did in the previous cycle. Most of your energy should be devoted to strength training. If you participate in spring ball or a spring sport (baseball, track, etc.), you will have to modify the program. See your coach and find a happy medium so you can participate in your sport and continue your physical development.

WORKOUT GOALS

Enter your new personal best for the exercises that were tested. Also, enter the calculated personal best for all of the other exercises. Remember, the numbers should represent one *single* repetition personal best.

Now set the goals you want to achieve by the end of the cycle. Be reasonable in setting goals. Make them challenging but obtainable. Your goals will be used to calculate how heavily you will train during this cycle.

As for your auxiliary exercises, use moderate weights at first (based on what you have done in the past) and progress when you can, following the direction in chapter 4.

Exercise	Personal Best	New Personal Goal
Bench press	_____	_____
Back squat	_____	_____
Power clean	_____	_____
Incline press	_____	_____
Behind-the-neck press	_____	_____
Dead lift	_____	_____

WORKOUT CHARTS

Pages 38-51 contain the workout charts you'll follow for the second off-season workout. You may choose either the split routine (MTuThF) or the total-body routine (MWF).

Off-Season II
Split Routine
Mondays

Exercise	Week 1	Week 2	Week 3	Week 4	Week 5
Date:	_____	_____	_____	_____	_____
Bench press	___ × 10	___ × 10	___ × 10	___ × 10	___ × 10
	___ × 10	___ × 8	___ × 8	___ × 8	___ × 8
	___ × 10	___ × 8	___ × 8	___ × 6	___ × 6
	___ × 10 (55%)	___ × 8	___ × 8	___ × 6	___ × 6
		___ × 8 (65%)	___ × 8 (68%)	___ × 6 (70%)	___ × 6 (72%)
Behind-the-neck press	___ × 10	___ × 10	___ × 10	___ × 10	___ × 10
	___ × 10	___ × 8	___ × 8	___ × 8	___ × 8
	___ × 10 (50%)	___ × 8	___ × 8	___ × 6	___ × 6
		___ × 8 (55%)	___ × 8 (58%)	___ × 6 (60%)	___ × 6 (62%)
Dumbbell flys	___ × 10	___ × 10	___ × 10	___ × 10	___ × 10
	___ × 10	___ × 10	___ × 10	___ × 8	___ × 8
	___ × 10	___ × 10	___ × 10	___ × 8	___ × 8
Bent-over rows	___ × 10	___ × 10	___ × 10	___ × 10	___ × 10
	___ × 10	___ × 10	___ × 10	___ × 8	___ × 8
	___ × 10	___ × 10	___ × 10	___ × 8	___ × 8
Bicep curls	___ × 10	___ × 10	___ × 10	___ × 10	___ × 10
	___ × 10	___ × 10	___ × 10	___ × 8	___ × 8
	___ × 10	___ × 10	___ × 10	___ × 8	___ × 8
Tricep extensions	___ × 10	___ × 10	___ × 10	___ × 10	___ × 10
	___ × 10	___ × 10	___ × 10	___ × 8	___ × 8
	___ × 10	___ × 10	___ × 10	___ × 8	___ × 8
Wrist curls	___ × 10	___ × 10	___ × 10	___ × 10	___ × 10
	___ × 10	___ × 10	___ × 10	___ × 8	___ × 8

Additional exercises:

Date:	_____	_____	_____	_____	_____
Exercise	**Week 6**	**Week 7**	**Week 8**	**Week 9**	**Week 10** **Test week**
Bench press	___× 10	___× 10	___× 10	___× 10	
	___× 8	___× 8	___× 8	___× 8	
	___× 6	___× 6	___× 6	___× 5	
	___× 6	___× 5	___× 5	___× 4 (85%)	
	___× 6 (75%)	___× 5 (78%)	___× 5 (80%)		
Behind-the-neck press	___× 10	___× 10	___× 10	___× 8	
	___× 8	___× 8	___× 8	___× 8	
	___× 6	___× 6	___× 6	___× 5	
	___× 6 (60%)	___× 5 (68%)	___× 5 (70%)	___× 3 (85%)	
Dumbbell flys	___× 10	___× 10	___× 10	___× 10	
	___× 8	___× 8	___× 8	___× 8	
	___× 8	___× 6	___× 6	___× 6	
Bent-over rows	___× 10	___× 10	___× 10	___× 10	
	___× 8	___× 8	___× 8	___× 8	
	___× 8	___× 6	___× 6	___× 6	
Bicep curls	___× 10	___× 10	___× 10	___× 10	
	___× 8	___× 8	___× 8	___× 8	
	___× 8	___× 6	___× 6	___× 6	
Tricep extensions	___× 10	___× 8	___× 8	___× 8	
	___× 8	___× 6	___× 6	___× 6	
	___× 8	___× 6	___× 6	___× 6	
Wrist curls	___× 10	___× 8	___× 8	___× 8	
	___× 8	___× 6	___× 6	___× 6	

Additional exercises:

Off-Season II
Split Routine
Tuesdays

Date:	_____	_____	_____	_____	_____
Exercise	**Week 1**	**Week 2**	**Week 3**	**Week 4**	**Week 5**
Back squat	___× 10	___× 10	___× 10	___× 10	___× 10
	___× 10	___× 8	___× 8	___× 8	___× 8
	___× 10	___× 8	___× 5	___× 5	___× 5
	___× 10 (55%)	___× 8 (70%)	___× 4	___× 4	___× 3
			___× 6 (75%)	___× 6 (78%)	___× 5 (82%)
			___× 8 (− 40)	___× 8 (− 40)	___× 6 (− 30)
			___× 8 (− 40)	___× 8 (− 40)	___× 6 (− 30)
Dead lift	___× 10	___× 10	___× 10	___× 10	___× 10
	___× 10	___× 8	___× 8	___× 8	___× 8
	___× 10 (50%)	___× 8	___× 8	___× 6	___× 6
		___× 8 (52%)	___× 8 (55%)	___× 6 (60%)	___× 6 (62%)
Leg curls	___× 10	___× 10	___× 10	___× 10	___× 10
	___× 10	___× 10	___× 10	___× 8	___× 8
	___× 10	___× 10	___× 10	___× 8	___× 8
Standing heel raises	___× 10	___× 10	___× 10	___× 10	___× 10
	___× 10	___× 10	___× 10	___× 8	___× 8
	___× 10	___× 10	___× 10	___× 8	___× 8
Oblique twists	___× 10	___× 10	___× 10	___× 10	___× 10
	___× 10	___× 10	___× 10	___× 8	___× 8
	___× 10	___× 10	___× 10	___× 8	___× 8
Neck resistance	___× 10	___× 10	___× 10	___× 10	___× 10
	___× 10	___× 10	___× 10	___× 8	___× 8
Sit-up crunch	___×___	___×___	___×___	___×___	___×___
	___×___	___×___	___×___	___×___	___×___
	___×___	___×___	___×___	___×___	___×___

Additional exercises:

Exercise	Week 6	Week 7	Week 8	Week 9	Week 10 Test week
Date:	_____	_____	_____	_____	_____
Back squat	___× 10	___× 10	___× 10	___× 10	
	___× 8	___× 8	___× 8	___× 8	
	___× 5	___× 5	___× 5	___× 5	
	___× 3	___× 3	___× 2	___× 2	
	___× 5 (85%)	___× 4 (88%)	___× 3 (90%)	___× 2 (92%)	
	___× 6 (− 30)	___× 5 (− 30)	___× 5 (− 40)		
	___× 6 (− 30)	___× 5 (− 30)	___× 5 (− 40)		
Dead lift	___× 10	___× 10	___× 10	___× 10	
	___× 8	___× 8	___× 8	___× 8	
	___× 6	___× 6	___× 6	___× 6	
	___× 6 (65%)	___× 5 (68%)	___× 5 (70%)	___× 5 (75%)	
Leg curls	___× 10	___× 10	___× 10	___× 10	
	___× 8	___× 8	___× 8	___× 8	
	___× 8	___× 6	___× 6	___× 6	
Standing heel raises	___× 10	___× 10	___× 10	___× 10	
	___× 8	___× 8	___× 8	___× 8	
	___× 8	___× 6	___× 6	___× 6	
Oblique twists	___× 10	___× 10	___× 10	___× 10	
	___× 8	___× 8	___× 8	___× 8	
	___× 8	___× 6	___× 6	___× 6	
Neck resistance	___× 10	___× 8	___× 8	___× 8	
	___× 8	___× 6	___× 6	___× 6	
Sit-up crunch	___×___	___×___	___×___	___×___	
	___×___	___×___	___×___	___×___	
	___×___	___×___	___×___	___×___	

Additional exercises:

Off-Season II
Split Routine
Thursdays

Exercise	Week 1	Week 2	Week 3	Week 4	Week 5
Date:	_____	_____	_____	_____	_____
Bench press	___× 10	___× 10	___× 10	___× 10	___× 10
	___× 10	___× 8	___× 8	___× 8	___× 8
	___× 10	___× 8	___× 5	___× 5	___× 5
	___× 10 (60%)	___× 8	___× 4	___× 4	___× 3
		___× 8 (70%)	___× 6 (75%)	___× 6 (78%)	___× 5 (82%)
			___× 8 (− 30)	___× 8 (− 30)	___× 6 (− 20)
			___× 8 (− 30)	___× 8 (− 30)	___× 6 (− 20)
Incline press	___× 10	___× 10	___× 10	___× 10	___× 10
	___× 10	___× 8	___× 8	___× 8	___× 8
	___× 10 (50%)	___× 8	___× 8	___× 6	___× 6
		___× 8 (52%)	___× 8 (55%)	___× 6 (60%)	___× 6 (62%)
Shoulder shrugs	___× 10	___× 10	___× 10	___× 10	___× 10
	___× 10	___× 10	___× 10	___× 8	___× 8
	___× 10	___× 10	___× 10	___× 8	___× 8
Bent-over rows	___× 10	___× 10	___× 10	___× 10	___× 10
	___× 10	___× 10	___× 10	___× 8	___× 8
	___× 10	___× 10	___× 10	___× 8	___× 8
Bicep curls	___× 10	___× 10	___× 10	___× 10	___× 10
	___× 10	___× 10	___× 10	___× 8	___× 8
	___× 10	___× 10	___× 10	___× 8	___× 8
Dips	___×___	___×___	___×___	___×___	___×___
	___×___	___×___	___×___	___×___	___×___

Additional exercises:

Off-Season II
Split Routine
Thursdays (continued)

Date:	_____	_____	_____	_____	_____
Exercise	Week 6	Week 7	Week 8	Week 9	Week 10 Test week
Bench press	___× 10	___× 10	___× 10	___× 10	
	___× 8	___× 8	___× 8	___× 8	
	___× 5	___× 5	___× 5	___× 5	
	___× 3	___× 3	___× 3	___× 2	
	___× 5 (85%)	___× 4 (88%)	___× 3 (90%)	___× 2 (92%)	
	___× 6 (− 20)	___× 5 (− 20)	___× 5 (− 30)		
	___× 6 (− 20)	___× 5 (− 20)	___× 5 (− 30)		
Incline press	___× 10	___× 10	___× 10	___× 10	
	___× 8	___× 8	___× 8	___× 8	
	___× 6	___× 6	___× 6	___× 5	
	___× 6 (65%)	___× 5 (68%)	___× 5 (70%)	___× 3 (75%)	
Shoulder shrugs	___× 10	___× 10	___× 10		
	___× 8	___× 8	___× 8		
	___× 8	___× 6	___× 6		
Bent-over rows	___× 10	___× 10	___× 10		
	___× 8	___× 8	___× 8		
	___× 8	___× 6	___× 6		
Bicep curls	___× 10	___× 10	___× 10		
	___× 8	___× 8	___× 8		
	___× 8	___× 6	___× 6		
Dips	___×___	___×___	___×___	___×___	
	___×___	___×___	___×___	___×___	

Additional exercises:

Off-Season II
Split Routine
Fridays

Exercise	Week 1	Week 2	Week 3	Week 4	Week 5
Date:	_____	_____	_____	_____	_____
Back squat	___× 10	___× 10	___× 10	___× 10	___× 10
	___× 10	___× 8	___× 8	___× 8	___× 8
	___× 10	___× 8	___× 8	___× 6	___× 6
	___× 10 (55%)	___× 8	___× 8	___× 6	___× 6
		___× 8 (58%)	___× 8 (60%)	___× 6 (65%)	___× 6 (68%)
Power clean	___× 8	___× 8	___× 8	___× 8	___× 8
	___× 5	___× 5	___× 5	___× 5	___× 5
	___× 5 (60%)	___× 5	___× 5	___× 4	___× 4
		___× 5 (65%)	___× 5 (68%)	___× 4 (72%)	___× 4 (75%)
Walking lunge (each leg)	___× 6	___× 6	___× 6	___× 5	___× 5
	___× 6	___× 6	___× 6	___× 5	___× 5
	___× 6	___× 6	___× 6	___× 5	___× 5
Leg curls	___× 10	___× 10	___× 10	___× 10	___× 10
	___× 10	___× 10	___× 10	___× 8	___× 8
	___× 10	___× 10	___× 10	___× 8	___× 8
Back raises	___× 10	___× 10	___× 10	___× 10	___× 10
	___× 10	___× 10	___× 10	___× 8	___× 8
	___× 10	___× 10	___× 10	___× 8	___× 8
Neck resistance	___× 10	___× 10	___× 10	___× 10	___× 10
	___× 10	___× 10	___× 10	___× 8	___× 8
Sit-up crunch	___×___	___×___	___×___	___×___	___×___
	___×___	___×___	___×___	___×___	___×___

Additional exercises:

Exercise	Week 6	Week 7	Week 8	Week 9	Week 10 Test week
Date:	_____	_____	_____	_____	_____
Back squat	___× 10	___× 10	___× 10	___× 10	
	___× 8	___× 8	___× 8	___× 8	
	___× 6	___× 6	___× 6	___× 5	
	___× 6	___× 5	___× 5	___× 3 (85%)	
	___× 6 (72%)	___× 5 (75%)	___× 5 (80%)		
Power clean	___× 5	___× 5	___× 5	___× 5	
	___× 5	___× 5	___× 5	___× 5	
	___× 4	___× 4	___× 3	___× 3	
	___× 3 (80%)	___× 3 (82%)	___× 3 (85%)	___× 2 (90%)	
Walking lunge (each leg)	___× 5	___× 4	___× 4		
	___× 5	___× 4	___× 4		
	___× 5	___× 4	___× 4		
Leg curls	___× 10	___× 10	___× 10		
	___× 8	___× 8	___× 8		
	___× 8	___× 6	___× 6		
Back raises	___× 10	___× 10	___× 10		
	___× 8	___× 8	___× 8		
	___× 8	___× 6	___× 6		
Neck resistance	___× 10	___× 8	___× 8		
	___× 8	___× 6	___× 6		
Sit-up crunch	___×___	___×___	___×___		
	___×___	___×___	___×___		

Additional exercises:

Off-Season II
Total-Body Routine
Mondays

Date:	————	————	————	————	————
Exercise	**Week 1**	**Week 2**	**Week 3**	**Week 4**	**Week 5**
Bench press	___× 10	___× 10	___× 10	___× 10	___× 10
	___× 10	___× 8	___× 8	___× 8	___× 8
	___× 10	___× 8	___× 5	___× 5	___× 5
	___× 10 (55%)	___× 8	___× 4	___× 4	___× 3
		___× 8 (65%)	___× 6 (75%)	___× 6 (78%)	___× 5 (82%)
			___× 8 (− 30)	___× 8 (− 30)	___× 6 (− 20)
			___× 8 (− 30)	___× 8 (− 30)	___× 6 (− 20)
Back squat	___× 10	___× 10	___× 10	___× 10	___× 10
	___× 10	___× 8	___× 8	___× 8	___× 8
	___× 10	___× 8	___× 8	___× 8	___× 6
	___× 10 (55%)	___× 8	___× 8	___× 8	___× 6
		___× 8 (60%)	___× 8 (65%)	___× 8 (68%)	___× 6 (70%)
Behind-the-neck press	___× 10	___× 10	___× 10	___× 10	___× 10
	___× 10	___× 8	___× 8	___× 8	___× 8
	___× 10 (50%)	___× 8	___× 8	___× 6	___× 6
		___× 8 (55%)	___× 8 (58%)	___× 6 (60%)	___× 6 (62%)
Shoulder shrugs	___× 10	___× 10	___× 10	___× 10	___× 10
	___× 10	___× 10	___× 10	___× 8	___× 8
	___× 10	___× 10	___× 10	___× 8	___× 8
Bent-over rows	___× 10	___× 10	___× 10	___× 10	___× 10
	___× 10	___× 10	___× 10	___× 8	___× 8
	___× 10	___× 10	___× 10	___× 8	___× 8
Bicep curls	___× 10	___× 10	___× 10	___× 10	___× 10
	___× 10	___× 10	___× 10	___× 8	___× 8
	___× 10	___× 10	___× 10	___× 8	___× 8
Oblique twists	___× 10	___× 10	___× 10	___× 10	___× 10
	___× 10	___× 10	___× 10	___× 8	___× 8
Neck resistance	___× 10	___× 10	___× 10	___× 10	___× 10
	___× 10	___× 10	___× 10	___× 8	___× 8
Sit-up crunch	___×___	___×___	___×___	___×___	___×___
	___×___	___×___	___×___	___×___	___×___
	___×___	___×___	___×___	___×___	___×___

Additional exercises:

Off-Season II
Total-Body Routine
Mondays (continued)

Exercise	Week 6	Week 7	Week 8	Week 9	Week 10 Test week
Date:	_____	_____	_____	_____	_____
Bench press	___× 10	___× 10	___× 10	___× 10	
	___× 8	___× 8	___× 8	___× 8	
	___× 5	___× 5	___× 5	___× 5	
	___× 3	___× 2	___× 2	___× 2	
	___× 5 (85%)	___× 4 (88%)	___× 3 (90%)	___× 2 (92%)	
	___× 6 (− 20)	___× 5 (− 20)	___× 5 (− 30)		
	___× 6 (− 20)	___× 5 (− 20)	___× 5 (− 30)		
Back squat	___× 10	___× 10	___× 10	___× 10	
	___× 8	___× 8	___× 8	___× 8	
	___× 6	___× 6	___× 6	___× 6	
	___× 6	___× 5	___× 5	___× 5	
	___× 6 (75%)	___× 5 (77%)	___× 5 (80%)	___× 5 (82%)	
Behind-the-neck press	___× 10	___× 10	___× 10	___× 10	
	___× 8	___× 8	___× 8	___× 8	
	___× 6	___× 6	___× 6	___× 5	
	___× 6 (65%)	___× 5 (68%)	___× 5 (70%)	___× 3 (75%)	
Shoulder shrugs	___× 10	___× 10	___× 10	___× 10	
	___× 8	___× 8	___× 8	___× 8	
	___× 8	___× 6	___× 6	___× 6	
Bent-over rows	___× 10	___× 10	___× 10	___× 10	
	___× 8	___× 8	___× 8	___× 8	
	___× 8	___× 6	___× 6	___× 6	
Bicep curls	___× 10	___× 10	___× 10	___× 10	
	___× 8	___× 8	___× 8	___× 8	
	___× 8	___× 6	___× 6	___× 6	
Oblique twists	___× 10	___× 8	___× 8	___× 8	
	___× 8	___× 6	___× 6	___× 6	
Neck resistance	___× 10	___× 8	___× 8	___× 8	
	___× 8	___× 6	___× 6	___× 6	
Sit-up crunch	___×___	___×___	___×___	___×___	
	___×___	___×___	___×___	___×___	
	___×___	___×___	___×___	___×___	

Additional exercises:

Off-Season II
Total-Body Routine
Wednesdays

Date:					
Exercise	**Week 1**	**Week 2**	**Week 3**	**Week 4**	**Week 5**
Power clean	___× 8	___× 8	___× 8	___× 5	___× 5
	___× 5	___× 5	___× 5	___× 5	___× 5
	___× 5	___× 5	___× 5	___× 5	___× 5
	___× 5 (65%)	___× 5	___× 5	___× 4	___× 4
		___× 5 (70%)	___× 5 (75%)	___× 4 (78%)	___× 4 (80%)
Incline press	___× 10	___× 10	___× 10	___× 10	___× 10
	___× 10	___× 10	___× 8	___× 8	___× 8
	___× 10	___× 10	___× 8	___× 8	___× 8
	___× 10 (50%)	___× 10 (52%)	___× 8	___× 8	___× 8
			___× 8 (55%)	___× 8 (60%)	___× 8 (62%)
Dead lift	___× 10	___× 10	___× 10	___× 10	___× 10
	___× 10	___× 10	___× 8	___× 8	___× 8
	___× 10	___× 10	___× 8	___× 8	___× 8
	___× 10 (50%)	___× 10 (52%)	___× 8 (55%)	___× 8 (58%)	___× 8 (60%)
Shoulder shrugs	___× 10	___× 10	___× 10	___× 10	___× 10
	___× 10	___× 10	___× 10	___× 8	___× 8
	___× 10	___× 10	___× 10	___× 8	___× 8
Dumbbell flys	___× 10	___× 10	___× 10	___× 10	___× 10
	___× 10	___× 10	___× 10	___× 8	___× 8
	___× 10	___× 10	___× 10	___× 8	___× 8
Tricep extensions	___× 10	___× 10	___× 10	___× 8	___× 8
	___× 10	___× 10	___× 10	___× 8	___× 8
	___× 10	___× 10	___× 10	___× 8	___× 8
Oblique twists	___× 10	___× 10	___× 10	___× 10	___× 10
	___× 10	___× 10	___× 10	___× 8	___× 8
Wrist curls	___× 10	___× 10	___× 10	___× 10	___× 10
	___× 10	___× 10	___× 10	___× 8	___× 8

Additional exercises:

Off-Season II
Total-Body Routine
Wednesdays (continued)

Date:	_____	_____	_____	_____	_____
Exercise	**Week 6**	**Week 7**	**Week 8**	**Week 9**	**Week 10** **Test week**
Power clean	____× 5	____× 5	____× 5	____× 5	
	____× 5	____× 5	____× 5	____× 4	
	____× 4	____× 4	____× 4	____× 3	
	____× 3	____× 3	____× 3	____× 2 (92%)	
	____× 3 (85%)	____× 2 (88%)	____× 2 (90%)		
Incline press	____× 10	____× 10	____× 10	____× 10	
	____× 8	____× 8	____× 8	____× 8	
	____× 6	____× 6	____× 6	____× 6	
	____× 6	____× 6	____× 5	____× 5	
	____× 6 (65%)	____× 6 (68%)	____× 5 (70%)	____× 5 (72%)	
Dead lift	____× 10	____× 10	____× 10	____× 10	
	____× 8	____× 8	____× 8	____× 8	
	____× 6	____× 6	____× 6	____× 6	
	____× 6 (62%)	____× 6 (65%)	____× 5 (68%)	____× 5 (70%)	
Shoulder shrugs	____× 10	____× 10	____× 10	____× 10	
	____× 8	____× 8	____× 8	____× 8	
	____× 8	____× 6	____× 6	____× 6	
Dumbbell flys	____× 10	____× 10	____× 10	____× 10	
	____× 8	____× 8	____× 8	____× 8	
	____× 8	____× 6	____× 6	____× 6	
Tricep extensions	____× 10	____× 10	____× 10	____× 10	
	____× 10	____× 8	____× 8	____× 8	
	____× 8	____× 6	____× 6	____× 6	
Oblique twists	____× 10	____× 8	____× 8	____× 8	
	____× 8	____× 6	____× 6	____× 6	
Wrist curls	____× 10	____× 8	____× 8	____× 8	
	____× 8	____× 6	____× 6	____× 6	

Additional exercises:

Off-Season II
Total-Body Routine
Fridays

Date: _____ _____ _____ _____ _____

Exercise	Week 1	Week 2	Week 3	Week 4	Week 5
Back squat	___× 10	___× 10	___× 10	___× 10	___× 10
	___× 10	___× 8	___× 8	___× 8	___× 8
	___× 10	___× 8	___× 5	___× 5	___× 5
	___× 10 (60%)	___× 8	___× 4	___× 4	___× 3
		___× 8 (65%)	___× 6 (72%)	___× 6 (78%)	___× 5 (82%)
			___× 8 (− 40)	___× 8 (− 40)	___× 6 (− 30)
			___× 8 (− 40)	___× 8 (− 40)	___× 6 (− 30)
Bench press	___× 10	___× 10	___× 10	___× 10	___× 10
	___× 10	___× 8	___× 8	___× 8	___× 8
	___× 10	___× 8	___× 8	___× 8	___× 8
	___× 10 (60%)	___× 8	___× 8	___× 8	___× 8
		___× 8 (65%)	___× 8 (68%)	___× 8 (70%)	___× 8 (72%)
Power clean	___× 8	___× 5	___× 5	___× 5	___× 5
	___× 6	___× 5	___× 5	___× 5	___× 5
	___× 5	___× 5	___× 5	___× 4	___× 4
	___× 5 (60%)	___× 5 (65%)	___× 5 (70%)	___× 4 (72%)	___× 4 (75%)
Alternate incline dumb-bell presses	___× 10	___× 10	___× 10	___× 10	___× 10
	___× 10	___× 10	___× 10	___× 8	___× 8
	___× 10	___× 10	___× 10	___× 8	___× 8
Bent-over rows	___× 10	___× 10	___× 10	___× 10	___× 10
	___× 10	___× 10	___× 10	___× 8	___× 8
	___× 10	___× 10	___× 10	___× 8	___× 8
Leg curls	___× 10	___× 10	___× 10	___× 10	___× 10
	___× 10	___× 10	___× 10	___× 8	___× 8
	___× 10	___× 10	___× 10	___× 8	___× 8
Bicep curls	___× 10	___× 10	___× 10	___× 10	___× 10
	___× 10	___× 10	___× 10	___× 8	___× 8
	___× 10	___× 10	___× 10	___× 8	___× 8
Neck resistance	___× 10	___× 10	___× 10	___× 10	___× 10
	___× 10	___× 10	___× 10	___× 8	___× 8
Sit-up crunch	___×___	___×___	___×___	___×___	___×___
	___×___	___×___	___×___	___×___	___×___

Additional exercises:

Off-Season II
Total-Body Routine
Fridays (continued)

Exercise	Week 6	Week 7	Week 8	Week 9	Week 10 Test week
Date:	_____	_____	_____	_____	_____
Back squat	___× 10	___× 10	___× 10	___× 10	
	___× 8	___× 8	___× 8	___× 8	
	___× 5	___× 5	___× 5	___× 5	
	___× 3	___× 2	___× 2	___× 2	
	___× 5 (85%)	___× 4 (88%)	___× 3 (90%)	___× 3 (92%)	
	___× 6 (− 30)	___× 5 (− 30)	___× 5 (− 40)		
	___× 6 (− 30)	___× 5 (− 30)	___× 5 (− 40)		
Bench press	___× 10	___× 10	___× 10	___× 10	
	___× 8	___× 8	___× 8	___× 8	
	___× 6	___× 6	___× 6	___× 6	
	___× 6	___× 6	___× 5	___× 5	
	___× 6 (75%)	___× 6 (78%)	___× 5 (80%)	___× 5 (82%)	
Power clean	___× 5	___× 5	___× 5	___× 5	
	___× 5	___× 4	___× 4	___× 4	
	___× 4	___× 3	___× 3	___× 3	
	___× 4 (78%)	___× 3 (80%)	___× 2 (82%)	___× 2 (85%)	
Alternate incline dumb-bell presses	___× 10	___× 10	___× 10		
	___× 8	___× 8	___× 8		
	___× 8	___× 6	___× 6		
Bent-over rows	___× 10	___× 10	___× 10		
	___× 8	___× 8	___× 8		
	___× 8	___× 6	___× 6		
Leg curls	___× 10	___× 10	___× 10		
	___× 8	___× 8	___× 8		
	___× 8	___× 6	___× 6		
Bicep curls	___× 10	___× 10	___× 10		
	___× 8	___× 8	___× 8		
	___× 8	___× 6	___× 6		
Neck resistance	___× 10	___× 10	___× 10		
	___× 8	___× 6	___× 6		
Sit-up crunch	___×___	___×___	___×___		
	___×___	___×___	___×___		

Additional exercises:

TEST WEEK

The 10th week of each routine is devoted to testing. Use the following guidelines and the chart provided while testing your progress.

1. Test in the presence of your coach.
2. Review the section on testing in chapter 4.
3. Choose between single max and rep max testing methods.
4. Record your goal weight.
5. Using the core exercise weight progression chart in Appendix B, fill in the weights for the warm-up sets leading up to your heavy set, just as you would do for a regular workout.
6. If during single max testing you reach your goal and think you can do more, try another single with a 5- to 10-lb increase.

7. For rep max testing do as many reps as you can with the final weight. If you can do more than five reps, great. Determine your calculated personal best using the personal best conversion chart in Appendix D.
8. If you are lifting very heavy weights, you may need more warm-up sets.
9. For your other core exercises that you are not actually testing (e.g., incline press), take your latest workout weight and use Appendix D to determine your calculated personal best.
10. Remember, you do not need to test auxiliary exercises.
11. If you have met your goals, great. If you've surpassed them, even better. If you did not reach your goals, reevaluate your goal-setting procedures.

SINGLE MAX TESTING

Power clean	Bench press	Back squat
_____ × 5	_____ × 8	_____ × 8
_____ × 3	_____ × 5	_____ × 5
_____ × 2	_____ × 3	_____ × 3
_____ × 1	_____ × 2	_____ × 2
_____ × 1 (goal)	_____ × 1	_____ × 1
	_____ × 1 (goal)	_____ × 1 (goal)

REP MAX TESTING

Power clean	Bench press	Back squat
_____ × 5	_____ × 8	_____ × 8
_____ × 3	_____ × 5	_____ × 5
_____ × 2	_____ × 3	_____ × 3
_____ × 3 (90% of goal)	_____ × 5 (85% of goal)	_____ × 5 (85% of goal)

Preseason Workout

This third and last cycle preparing you for the upcoming season should start in early summer and end just before football practice starts in August. Family vacations often conflict with this cycle. Do your best in that situation. Refer to the section "What If I Miss Training Days?" in chapter 4.

The sample workout is for 9 weeks of training plus 1 week of testing. If your summer schedule allows only 7 weeks, delete Weeks 2 and 4. If you have only 8 weeks, delete Week 2 from the program. Remember to consult with your coach when modifying your workout plan.

At this time of the year, you should also work on conditioning, speed, agility, and perfecting your football skill. Remember, you must be a total athlete to be a good football player.

WORKOUT GOALS

Record your new personal best for the exercises that were tested, and record the calculated personal best for all of the other exercises. Remember, the number should represent one *single* repetition personal best.

Now set the goals you want to achieve by the end of this cycle. Be reasonable in setting goals. Make them challenging but obtainable. Your goals will be used to calculate how heavily you will train during this cycle. As for your auxiliary exercises, use moderate weights at first (based on what you have done in the past) and progress when you can, following the direction in chapter 4.

Exercise	Personal Best	New Personal Goal
Bench press	_____	_____
Back squat	_____	_____
Power clean	_____	_____
Incline press	_____	_____
Behind-the-neck press	_____	_____

WORKOUT CHARTS

Pages 54-67 contain the workout charts you'll follow for the preseason workout. You may choose either the split routine (MTuThF) or the total-body routine (MWF).

Preseason
Split Routine
Mondays

Date:	_____	_____	_____	_____	_____
Exercise	**Week 1**	**Week 2**	**Week 3**	**Week 4**	**Week 5**
Bench press	___× 10	___× 10	___× 10	___× 10	___× 10
	___× 10	___× 8	___× 8	___× 8	___× 8
	___× 10	___× 8	___× 8	___× 6	___× 6
	___× 10 (55%)	___× 8	___× 8	___× 6	___× 6
		___× 8 (62%)	___× 8 (68%)	___× 6 (72%)	___× 6 (75%)
Incline press	___× 10	___× 10	___× 10	___× 10	___× 10
	___× 10	___× 8	___× 8	___× 8	___× 8
	___× 10 (55%)	___× 8	___× 8	___× 6	___× 6
		___× 8 (60%)	___× 8 (65%)	___× 6 (68%)	___× 6 (70%)
Shoulder shrugs	___× 10	___× 10	___× 10	___× 10	___× 10
	___× 10	___× 10	___× 10	___× 8	___× 8
	___× 10	___× 10	___× 10	___× 8	___× 8
Dumbbell flys	___× 10	___× 10	___× 10	___× 10	___× 10
	___× 10	___× 10	___× 10	___× 8	___× 8
	___× 10	___× 10	___× 10	___× 8	___× 8
Bicep curls	___× 10	___× 10	___× 10	___× 10	___× 10
	___× 10	___× 10	___× 10	___× 8	___× 8
	___× 10	___× 10	___× 10	___× 8	___× 8
Tricep extensions	___× 10	___× 10	___× 10	___× 10	___× 10
	___× 10	___× 10	___× 10	___× 8	___× 8
	___× 10	___× 10	___× 10	___× 8	___× 8

Additional exercises:

Preseason
Split Routine
Mondays (continued)

Date:	_____	_____	_____	_____	_____
Exercise	**Week 6**	**Week 7**	**Week 8**	**Week 9**	**Week 10** **Test week**
Bench press	___× 10	___× 10	___× 10	___× 8	
	___× 8	___× 8	___× 8	___× 6	
	___× 6	___× 6	___× 5	___× 5	
	___× 5	___× 5	___× 3	___× 3 (85%)	
	___× 5 (77%)	___× 5 (80%)	___× 3 (82%)		
Incline press	___× 10	___× 10	___× 10	___× 10	
	___× 8	___× 8	___× 8	___× 8	
	___× 8	___× 8	___× 8	___× 6	
	___× 5 (72%)	___× 5 (75%)	___× 3 (77%)	___× 3 (80%)	
Shoulder shrugs	___× 10	___× 10	___× 10	___× 10	
	___× 8	___× 8	___× 8	___× 8	
	___× 8	___× 6	___× 6	___× 6	
Dumbbell flys	___× 10	___× 10	___× 10	___× 10	
	___× 8	___× 8	___× 8	___× 8	
	___× 8	___× 6	___× 6	___× 6	
Bicep curls	___× 10	___× 10	___× 10	___× 10	
	___× 8	___× 8	___× 8	___× 8	
	___× 8	___× 6	___× 6	___× 6	
Tricep extensions	___× 10	___× 10	___× 10	___× 10	
	___× 8	___× 8	___× 8	___× 8	
	___× 8	___× 6	___× 6	___× 6	

Additional exercises:

Preseason
Split Routine
Tuesdays

Date:	_____	_____	_____	_____	_____
Exercise	**Week 1**	**Week 2**	**Week 3**	**Week 4**	**Week 5**
Back squat	___× 10	___× 10	___× 10	___× 10	___× 10
	___× 10	___× 8	___× 8	___× 8	___× 8
	___× 10	___× 5	___× 5	___× 5	___× 5
	___× 10 (55%)	___× 3	___× 3	___× 3	___× 3
		___× 8 (62%)	___× 6 (75%)	___× 6 (80%)	___× 5 (82%)
			___× 8 (− 20)	___× 8 (− 20)	___× 8 (− 30)
			___× 8 (− 20)	___× 8 (− 20)	___× 8 (− 30)
Power clean	___× 8	___× 8	___× 8	___× 5	___× 5
	___× 5	___× 5	___× 5	___× 5	___× 5
	___× 5	___× 5	___× 5	___× 5	___× 5
	___× 5 (55%)	___× 5 (65%)	___× 5 (70%)	___× 4 (72%)	___× 4 (75%)
Walking lunge (each leg)	___× 6	___× 6	___× 6	___× 5	___× 5
	___× 6	___× 6	___× 6	___× 5	___× 5
	___× 6	___× 6	___× 6	___× 5	___× 5
Back raises	___× 10	___× 10	___× 10	___× 10	___× 10
	___× 10	___× 10	___× 10	___× 8	___× 8
	___× 10	___× 10	___× 10	___× 8	___× 8
Oblique twists	___× 10	___× 10	___× 10	___× 10	___× 10
	___× 10	___× 10	___× 10	___× 8	___× 8
	___× 10	___× 10	___× 10	___× 8	___× 8
Neck resistance	___× 10	___× 10	___× 10	___× 10	___× 10
	___× 10	___× 10	___× 10	___× 8	___× 8
Sit-up crunch	___×___	___×___	___×___	___×___	___×___
	___×___	___×___	___×___	___×___	___×___
	___×___	___×___	___×___	___×___	___×___

Additional exercises:

Preseason
Split Routine
Tuesdays (continued)

Exercise	Week 6	Week 7	Week 8	Week 9	Week 10 Test week
Date:	_____	_____	_____	_____	_____
Back squat	____ × 10	____ × 10	____ × 8	____ × 8	
	____ × 8	____ × 8	____ × 6	____ × 5	
	____ × 5	____ × 5	____ × 3	____ × 3	
	____ × 2	____ × 2	____ × 1	____ × 2	
	____ × 4 (85%)	____ × 3 (90%)	____ × 2 (92%)	____ × 1 (95%)	
	____ × 6 (− 20)	____ × 5 (− 25)	____ × 4 (− 30)		
	____ × 6 (− 20)	____ × 5 (− 25)	____ × 4 (− 30)		
Power clean	____ × 5	____ × 5	____ × 5	____ × 5	
	____ × 5	____ × 5	____ × 5	____ × 5	
	____ × 4	____ × 4	____ × 3	____ × 3	
	____ × 3 (77%)	____ × 3 (80%)	____ × 2 (82%)	____ × 2 (85%)	
Walking lunge (each leg)	____ × 5	____ × 4	____ × 4	____ × 4	
	____ × 5	____ × 4	____ × 4	____ × 4	
	____ × 5	____ × 4	____ × 4	____ × 4	
Back raises	____ × 10	____ × 10	____ × 10	____ × 10	
	____ × 8	____ × 8	____ × 8	____ × 8	
	____ × 8	____ × 6	____ × 6	____ × 6	
Oblique twists	____ × 10	____ × 10	____ × 10	____ × 10	
	____ × 8	____ × 8	____ × 8	____ × 8	
	____ × 8	____ × 6	____ × 6	____ × 6	
Neck resistance	____ × 10	____ × 8	____ × 8	____ × 8	
	____ × 8	____ × 6	____ × 6	____ × 6	
Sit-up crunch	____ × ____	____ × ____	____ × ____	____ × ____	
	____ × ____	____ × ____	____ × ____	____ × ____	
	____ × ____	____ × ____	____ × ____	____ × ____	

Additional exercises:

Preseason
Split Routine
Thursdays

Exercise	Week 1	Week 2	Week 3	Week 4	Week 5
Date:	_____	_____	_____	_____	_____
Bench press	___× 10	___× 10	___× 10	___× 10	___× 10
	___× 10	___× 8	___× 8	___× 8	___× 8
	___× 10	___× 5	___× 5	___× 5	___× 5
	___× 10 (60%)	___× 3	___× 3	___× 3	___× 3
		___× 8 (70%)	___× 6 (75%)	___× 5 (80%)	___× 5 (85%)
			___× 8 (− 20)	___× 8 (− 20)	___× 8 (− 30)
			___× 8 (− 20)	___× 8 (− 20)	___× 8 (− 30)
Behind-the-neck press	___× 10	___× 10	___× 10	___× 10	___× 10
	___× 10	___× 8	___× 8	___× 8	___× 8
	___× 10	___× 8	___× 8	___× 6	___× 6
	___× 10 (50%)	___× 8 (55%)	___× 8 (60%)	___× 6 (62%)	___× 6 (65%)
Bent-over rows	___× 10	___× 10	___× 10	___× 10	___× 10
	___× 10	___× 10	___× 10	___× 8	___× 8
	___× 10	___× 10	___× 10	___× 8	___× 8
Bicep curls	___× 10	___× 10	___× 10	___× 10	___× 10
	___× 10	___× 10	___× 10	___× 8	___× 8
	___× 10	___× 10	___× 10	___× 8	___× 8
Wrist curls	___× 10	___× 10	___× 10	___× 10	___× 10
	___× 10	___× 10	___× 10	___× 8	___× 8
	___× 10	___× 10	___× 10	___× 8	___× 8
Dips	___×___	___×___	___×___	___×___	___×___
	___×___	___×___	___×___	___×___	___×___

Additional exercises:

Preseason
Split Routine
Thursdays (continued)

Date:	_____	_____	_____	_____	_____
Exercise	Week 6	Week 7	Week 8	Week 9	**Week 10** **Test week**
Bench press	___× 10	___× 10	___× 8	___× 8	
	___× 8	___× 8	___× 6	___×5	
	___× 5	___× 5	___× 3	___× 3	
	___× 2	___× 1	___× 1	___× 2	
	___× 4 (87%)	___× 3 (90%)	___× 2 (92%)	___× 1 (95%)	
	___× 6 (− 20)	___× 5 (− 25)	___× 4 (− 30)		
	___× 6 (− 20)	___× 5 (− 25)	___× 4 (− 30)		
Behind-the- neck press	___× 10	___× 10	___× 10	___× 10	
	___× 8	___× 8	___× 8	___× 8	
	___× 6	___× 6	___× 5	___× 5	
	___× 5 (68%)	___× 5 (70%)	___× 3 (72%)	___× 3 (75%)	
Bent-over rows	___× 10	___× 10	___× 10		
	___× 8	___× 8	___× 8		
	___× 8	___× 6	___× 6		
Bicep curls	___× 10	___× 10	___× 10		
	___× 8	___× 8	___× 8		
	___× 8	___× 6	___× 6		
Wrist curls	___× 10	___× 10	___× 10		
	___× 8	___× 8	___× 8		
	___× 8	___× 6	___× 6		
Dips	___×___	___×___	___×___		
	___×___	___×___	___×___		

Additional exercises:

Preseason
Split Routine
Fridays

Date:	_____	_____	_____	_____	_____
Exercise	**Week 1**	**Week 2**	**Week 3**	**Week 4**	**Week 5**
Power clean	___× 8	___× 8	___× 5	___× 5	___× 5
	___× 5	___× 5	___× 5	___× 5	___× 4
	___× 5	___× 5	___× 4	___× 4	___× 4
	___× 5 (65%)	___× 5	___× 4	___× 4	___× 3
		___× 5 (75%)	___× 4 (80%)	___× 4 (82%)	___× 3 (85%)
Back squat	___× 10	___× 10	___× 10	___× 10	___× 10
	___× 10	___× 8	___× 8	___× 8	___× 8
	___× 10	___× 8	___× 8	___× 6	___× 6
	___× 10 (60%)	___× 8	___× 8	___× 6	___× 6
		___× 8 (65%)	___× 8 (68%)	___× 6 (72%)	___× 6 (75%)
Walking lunge (each leg)	___× 6	___× 6	___× 6	___× 5	___× 5
	___× 6	___× 6	___× 6	___× 5	___× 5
	___× 6	___× 6	___× 6	___× 5	___× 5
Leg curls	___× 10	___× 10	___× 10	___× 10	___× 10
	___× 10	___× 10	___× 10	___× 8	___× 8
	___× 10	___× 10	___× 10	___× 8	___× 8
Standing heel raises	___× 10	___× 10	___× 10	___× 10	___× 10
	___× 10	___× 10	___× 10	___× 8	___× 8
	___× 10	___× 10	___× 10	___× 8	___× 8
Neck resistance	___× 10	___× 10	___× 10	___× 10	___× 10
	___× 10	___× 10	___× 10	___× 8	___× 8
Sit-up crunch	___×___	___×___	___×___	___×___	___×___
	___×___	___×___	___×___	___×___	___×___

Additional exercises:

Preseason
Split Routine
Fridays (continued)

Date:	____	____	____	____	____
Exercise	Week 6	Week 7	Week 8	Week 9	Week 10 Test week
Power clean	___ × 5	___ × 5	___ × 5	___ × 5	
	___ × 4	___ × 4	___ × 4	___ × 3	
	___ × 3	___ × 3	___ × 3	___ × 2	
	___ × 2	___ × 2	___ × 2	___ × 1 (95%)	
	___ × 2 (87%)	___ × 2 (90%)	___ × 1 (92%)		
Back squat	___ × 10	___ × 10	___ × 10	___ × 8	
	___ × 8	___ × 8	___ × 8	___ × 6	
	___ × 6	___ × 6	___ × 5	___ × 5	
	___ × 5	___ × 5	___ × 3	___ × 3 (85%)	
	___ × 5 (77%)	___ × 5 (80%)	___ × 3 (82%)		
Walking lunge (each leg)	___ × 5	___ × 4	___ × 4		
	___ × 5	___ × 4	___ × 4		
	___ × 5	___ × 4	___ × 4		
Leg curls	___ × 10	___ × 10	___ × 10		
	___ × 8	___ × 8	___ × 8		
	___ × 8	___ × 6	___ × 6		
Standing heel raises	___ × 10	___ × 10	___ × 10		
	___ × 8	___ × 8	___ × 8		
	___ × 8	___ × 6	___ × 6		
Neck resistance	___ × 10	___ × 8	___ × 8		
	___ × 8	___ × 6	___ × 6		
Sit-up crunch	___ × ___	___ × ___	___ × ___		
	___ × ___	___ × ___	___ × ___		

Additional exercises:

Preseason
Total-Body Routine
Mondays

Date:	_____	_____	_____	_____	_____
Exercise	**Week 1**	**Week 2**	**Week 3**	**Week 4**	**Week 5**
Bench press	___× 10	___× 10	___× 10	___× 10	___× 10
	___× 10	___× 8	___× 8	___× 8	___× 8
	___× 10	___× 5	___× 5	___× 5	___× 5
	___× 10 (60%)	___× 3	___× 3	___× 3	___× 3
		___× 8 (70%)	___× 6 (75%)	___× 5 (80%)	___× 5 (82%)
			___× 8 (− 20)	___× 8 (− 20)	___× 8 (− 30)
			___× 8 (− 20)	___× 8 (− 20)	___× 8 (− 30)
Back squat	___× 10	___× 10	___× 10	___× 10	___× 10
	___× 10	___× 8	___× 8	___× 8	___× 8
	___× 10	___× 8	___× 8	___× 6	___× 6
	___× 10 (55%)	___× 8	___× 8	___× 6	___× 6
		___× 8 (60%)	___× 8 (65%)	___× 6 (70%)	___× 6 (72%)
Incline press	___× 10	___× 10	___× 10	___× 10	___× 10
	___× 10	___× 8	___× 8	___× 8	___× 8
	___× 10	___× 8	___× 8	___× 6	___× 6
	___× 10 (55%)	___× 8 (58%)	___× 8 (60%)	___× 6 (62%)	___× 6 (65%)
Shoulder shrugs	___× 10	___× 10	___× 10	___× 10	___× 10
	___× 10	___× 10	___× 10	___× 8	___× 8
	___× 10	___× 10	___× 10	___× 8	___× 8
Bent-over rows	___× 10	___× 10	___× 10	___× 10	___× 10
	___× 10	___× 10	___× 10	___× 8	___× 8
	___× 10	___× 10	___× 10	___× 8	___× 8
Bicep curls	___× 10	___× 10	___× 10	___× 10	___× 10
	___× 10	___× 10	___× 10	___× 8	___× 8
	___× 10	___× 10	___× 10	___× 8	___× 8
Standing heel raises	___× 10	___× 10	___× 10	___× 10	___× 10
	___× 10	___× 10	___× 10	___× 8	___× 8
Neck resistance	___× 10	___× 10	___× 10	___× 10	___× 10
	___× 10	___× 10	___× 10	___× 8	___× 8
Sit-up crunch	___×___	___×___	___×___	___×___	___×___
	___×___	___×___	___×___	___×___	___×___
	___×___	___×___	___×___	___×___	___×___

Additional exercises:

Preseason
Total-Body Routine
Mondays (continued)

Exercise	Week 6	Week 7	Week 8	Week 9	Week 10 Test week
Date:	_____	_____	_____	_____	_____
Bench press	___× 10	___× 10	___× 8	___× 8	
	___× 8	___× 8	___× 6	___× 5	
	___× 5	___× 5	___× 3	___× 3	
	___× 2	___× 2	___× 1	___× 1	
	___× 4 (85%)	___× 3 (90%)	___× 2 (92%)	___× 1 (95%)	
	___× 6 (− 20)	___× 5 (− 20)	___× 4 (− 30)		
	___× 6 (− 20)	___× 5 (− 20)	___× 4 (− 30)		
Back squat	___× 10	___× 10	___× 10	___× 10	
	___× 8	___× 8	___× 8	___× 8	
	___× 6	___× 6	___× 5	___× 5	
	___× 5	___× 5	___× 3	___× 3	
	___× 5 (75%)	___× 3 (78%)	___× 3 (82%)	___× 3 (85%)	
Incline press	___× 10	___× 10	___× 10	___× 10	
	___× 8	___× 8	___× 8	___× 8	
	___× 8	___× 6	___× 5	___× 5	
	___× 5 (68%)	___× 5 (70%)	___× 3 (72%)	___× 3 (75%)	
Shoulder shrugs	___× 10	___× 10	___× 10	___× 10	
	___× 8	___× 6	___× 6	___× 6	
	___× 8	___× 6	___× 6	___× 6	
Bent-over rows	___× 10	___× 10	___× 10	___× 10	
	___× 8	___× 8	___× 8	___× 8	
	___× 8	___× 6	___× 6	___× 6	
Bicep curls	___× 10	___× 8	___× 8	___× 8	
	___× 8	___× 8	___× 8	___× 8	
	___× 8	___× 6	___× 6	___× 6	
Standing heel raises	___× 10	___× 8	___× 8	___× 8	
	___× 8	___× 6	___× 6	___× 6	
Neck resistance	___× 10	___× 8	___× 8	___× 8	
	___× 8	___× 6	___× 6	___× 6	
Sit-up crunch	___×___	___×___	___×___	___×___	
	___×___	___×___	___×___	___×___	
	___×___	___×___	___×___	___×___	

Additional exercises:

Preseason
Total-Body Routine
Wednesdays

Date:	_____	_____	_____	_____	_____
Exercise	**Week 1**	**Week 2**	**Week 3**	**Week 4**	**Week 5**
Power clean	____× 8	____× 8	____× 5	____× 5	____× 5
	____× 5	____× 5	____× 5	____× 5	____× 4
	____× 5	____× 5	____× 4	____× 4	____× 4
	____× 5 (60%)	____× 5	____× 4	____× 4	____× 3
		____× 5 (70%)	____× 4 (80%)	____× 4 (82%)	____× 3 (85%)
Behind-the-neck press	____× 10	____× 10	____× 10	____× 10	____× 10
	____× 10	____× 8	____× 8	____× 8	____× 8
	____× 10	____× 8	____× 8	____× 8	____× 6
	____× 10 (50%)	____× 8	____× 8	____× 8	____× 6
		____× 8 (55%)	____× 8 (57%)	____× 8 (60%)	____× 6 (62%)
Walking lunge (each leg)	____× 6	____× 6	____× 6	____× 5	____× 5
	____× 6	____× 6	____× 6	____× 5	____× 5
	____× 6	____× 6	____× 6	____× 5	____× 5
Dumbbell flys	____× 10	____× 10	____× 10	____× 10	____× 10
	____× 10	____× 10	____× 10	____× 8	____× 8
	____× 10	____× 10	____× 10	____× 8	____× 8
Shoulder shrugs	____× 10	____× 10	____× 10	____× 10	____× 10
	____× 10	____× 10	____× 10	____× 8	____× 8
	____× 10	____× 10	____× 10	____× 8	____× 8
Tricep extensions	____× 10	____× 10	____× 10	____× 8	____× 8
	____× 10	____× 10	____× 10	____× 8	____× 8
	____× 10	____× 10	____× 10	____× 8	____× 8
Leg curls	____× 10	____× 10	____× 10	____× 10	____× 10
	____× 10	____× 10	____× 10	____× 8	____× 8
Wrist curls	____× 10	____× 10	____× 10	____× 10	____× 10
	____× 10	____× 10	____× 10	____× 8	____× 8

Additional exercises:

Preseason
Total-Body Routine
Wednesdays (continued)

Date:	_____	_____	_____	_____	_____
Exercise	**Week 6**	**Week 7**	**Week 8**	**Week 9**	**Week 10** **Test week**
Power clean	____× 5	____× 5	____× 5	____× 5	
	____× 4	____× 4	____× 4	____× 3	
	____× 3	____× 3	____× 3	____× 2	
	____× 3	____× 3	____× 2	____× 1 (95%)	
	____× 2 (87%)	____× 2 (90%)	____× 2 (92%)		
Behind-the-neck press	____× 10	____× 10	____× 10	____× 10	
	____× 8	____× 8	____× 8	____× 8	
	____× 6	____× 6	____× 6	____× 6	
	____× 6	____× 6	____× 5	____× 5	
	____× 6 (65%)	____× 6 (68%)	____× 5 (70%)	____× 5 (72%)	
Walking lunge (each leg)	____× 5	____× 4	____× 4	____× 4	
	____× 5	____× 4	____× 4	____× 4	
	____× 5	____× 4	____× 4	____× 4	
Dumbbell flys	____× 10	____× 10	____× 10	____× 10	
	____× 8	____× 8	____× 8	____× 8	
	____× 8	____× 6	____× 6	____× 6	
Shoulder shrugs	____× 10	____× 10	____× 10	____× 10	
	____× 8	____× 8	____× 8	____× 8	
	____× 8	____× 6	____× 6	____× 6	
Tricep extensions	____× 10	____× 10	____× 10	____× 10	
	____× 8	____× 8	____× 8	____× 8	
	____× 8	____× 6	____× 6	____× 6	
Leg curls	____× 10	____× 8	____× 8	____× 8	
	____× 8	____× 6	____× 6	____× 6	
Wrist curls	____× 10	____× 8	____× 8	____× 8	
	____× 8	____× 6	____× 6	____× 6	

Additional exercises:

Preseason
Total-Body Routine
Fridays

Exercise	Week 1	Week 2	Week 3	Week 4	Week 5
Date:	_____	_____	_____	_____	_____
Back squat	___× 10	___× 10	___× 10	___× 10	___× 10
	___× 10	___× 8	___× 8	___× 8	___× 8
	___× 10	___× 5	___× 5	___× 5	___× 5
	___× 10 (60%)	___× 3	___× 3	___× 3	___× 3
		___× 8 (65%)	___× 6 (70%)	___× 6 (75%)	___× 5 (80%)
			___× 8 (− 40)	___× 8 (− 40)	___× 8 (− 40)
			___× 8 (− 40)	___× 8 (− 40)	___× 8 (− 40)
Power clean	___× 8	___× 8	___× 5	___× 5	___× 5
	___× 5	___× 5	___× 5	___× 5	___× 4
	___× 5	___× 5	___× 4	___× 4	___× 3
	___× 5 (60%)	___× 5 (65%)	___× 4 (68%)	___× 4 (70%)	___× 3 (72%)
Bench press	___× 10	___× 10	___× 10	___× 10	___× 10
	___× 10	___× 8	___× 8	___× 8	___× 8
	___× 10	___× 8	___× 8	___× 8	___× 6
	___× 10 (55%)	___× 8	___× 8	___× 8	___× 6
		___× 8 (60%)	___× 8 (62%)	___× 8 (65%)	___× 6 (70%)
Bent-over rows	___× 10	___× 10	___× 10	___× 10	___× 10
	___× 10	___× 10	___× 10	___× 8	___× 8
	___× 10	___× 10	___× 10	___× 8	___× 8
Alternate incline dumbbell presses	___× 10	___× 10	___× 10	___× 10	___× 10
	___× 10	___× 10	___× 10	___× 8	___× 8
	___× 10	___× 10	___× 10	___× 8	___× 8
Bicep curls	___× 10	___× 10	___× 10	___× 10	___× 10
	___× 10	___× 10	___× 10	___× 8	___× 8
	___× 10	___× 10	___× 10	___× 8	___× 8
Oblique twists	___× 10	___× 10	___× 10	___× 10	___× 10
	___× 10	___× 10	___× 10	___× 8	___× 8
Neck resistance	___× 10	___× 10	___× 10	___× 10	___× 10
	___× 10	___× 10	___× 10	___× 8	___× 8
Sit-up crunch	___×___	___×___	___×___	___×___	___×___
	___×___	___×___	___×___	___×___	___×___

Additional exercises:

Preseason
Total-Body Routine
Fridays (continued)

Date:	_____	_____	_____	_____	_____
Exercise	**Week 6**	**Week 7**	**Week 8**	**Week 9**	**Week 10** **Test week**
Back squat	___× 10	___× 10	___× 8	___× 8	
	___× 8	___× 8	___× 5	___× 5	
	___× 5	___× 5	___× 3	___× 3	
	___× 2	___× 2	___× 1	___× 1	
	___× 4 (85%)	___× 3 (90%)	___× 2 (92%)	___× 1 (95%)	
	___× 6 (− 40)	___× 5 (− 40)	___× 4 (− 40)		
	___× 6 (− 40)	___× 5 (− 40)	___× 4 (− 40)		
Power clean	___× 5	___× 5	___× 5	___× 5	
	___× 4	___× 4	___× 4	___× 4	
	___× 3	___× 3	___× 3	___× 3	
	___× 3 (75%)	___× 2 (78%)	___× 2 (80%)	___× 2 (85%)	
Bench press	___× 10	___× 10	___× 10	___× 10	
	___× 10	___× 8	___× 8	___× 8	
	___× 6	___× 6	___× 6	___× 6	
	___× 6	___× 6	___× 5	___× 5	
	___× 6 (72%)	___× 6 (75%)	___× 5 (78%)	___× 5 (80%)	
Bent-over rows	___× 10	___× 10	___× 10		
	___× 8	___× 8	___× 8		
	___× 8	___× 6	___× 6		
Alternate incline dumb-bell presses	___× 10	___× 10	___× 10		
	___× 8	___× 8	___× 8		
	___× 8	___× 6	___× 6		
Bicep curls	___× 10	___× 10	___× 10		
	___× 8	___× 8	___× 8		
	___× 8	___× 6	___× 6		
Oblique twists	___× 10	___× 10	___× 10		
	___× 8	___× 6	___× 6		
Neck resistance	___× 10	___× 8	___× 8		
	___× 8	___× 6	___× 6		
Sit-up crunch	___×___	___×___	___×___		
	___×___	___×___	___×___		

Additional exercises:

TEST WEEK

The 10th week of each routine is devoted to testing. Use the following guidelines and the chart provided while testing your progress.

1. Test in the presence of your coach.
2. Review the section on testing in chapter 4.
3. Choose between single max and rep max testing methods.
4. Record your goal weight.
5. Using the core exercise weight progression chart in Appendix B, fill in the weights for the warm-up sets leading up to your heavy set, just as you would do for a regular workout.
6. If during single max testing, you reach your goal and think you can do more, try another single with a 5- to 10-lb increase.
7. For rep max testing do as many reps as you can with the final weight. If you can do more than five reps, great. Determine your calculated personal best by using the personal best conversion chart (Appendix D).
8. If you are lifting very heavy weights, you may need more warm-up sets.
9. For your other core exercises that you are not actually testing (e.g., incline press), take your last workout weight and use Appendix D to determine your calculated personal best.
10. Remember, you do not need to test auxiliary exercises.
11. If you have met your goals, great. If you've surpassed them, even better. If you did not reach your goals, reevaluate your goal-setting procedures.

SINGLE MAX TESTING

Power clean	Bench press	Back squat
_____ × 5	_____ × 8	_____ × 8
_____ × 3	_____ × 5	_____ × 5
_____ × 2	_____ × 3	_____ × 3
_____ × 1	_____ × 2	_____ × 2
_____ × 1 (goal)	_____ × 1	_____ × 1
	_____ × 1 (goal)	_____ × 1 (goal)

REP MAX TESTING

Power clean	Bench press	Back squat
_____ × 5	_____ × 8	_____ × 8
_____ × 3	_____ × 5	_____ × 5
_____ × 2	_____ × 3	_____ × 3
_____ × 3 (90% of goal)	_____ × 5 (85% of goal)	_____ × 5 (85% of goal)

In-Season Workout

This training cycle should begin with the start of practice in August and end with the end of the football season.

The sample cycle is for 14 weeks. If your season lasts only 10 weeks, do not do the last 4 weeks. If your season lasts 12 weeks, do not do the last 2 weeks. Your main goal for this cycle is to maintain your strength level *throughout* the season. Some of you may be able to increase your strength level, especially in the upper body exercises. Again, consult with your coach before modifying the workout plan.

Because much time is spent on the practice field and in game preparation, I suggest you strength-train two times per week, training the total body each time.

WORKOUT GOALS

Record your new personal best for the exercises that were tested. Also, record the calculated personal best for all of the other exercises. Remember, the number should represent one *single* repetition personal best.

Because you aim to maintain strength throughout the season, your goal for each exercise should be the same as your personal best. Base your percentages for the season on your best performance of the preseason just completed.

Exercise	Personal Best	New Personal Goal
Bench press	_____	_____
Back squat	_____	_____
Power clean	_____	_____
Incline press	_____	_____
Behind-the-neck press	_____	_____
Leg press	_____	_____

WORKOUT CHARTS

Pages 70-75 contain the workout charts you'll follow during the season. They comprise a total-body routine (MW) that runs for 14 weeks. A split routine is not offered.

There is no need to have a test week at the end of the season unless you and your coach think it is important for your program.

To see if you have met your goals of maintaining a high level of strength throughout the season, use the workout weights for each exercise and Appendix D.

In-Season
Mondays

Date:	_____	_____	_____	_____	_____
Exercise	**Week 1**	**Week 2**	**Week 3**	**Week 4**	**Week 5**
Back squat	____× 10	____× 10	____× 10	____× 10	____× 10
	____× 8	____× 8	____× 8	____× 8	____× 8
	____× 8	____× 8	____× 8	____× 6	____× 6
	____× 8 (45%)	____× 8 (48%)	____× 8 (50%)	____× 6 (50%)	____× 6 (52%)
Bench press	____× 10	____× 10	____× 10	____× 10	____× 10
	____× 8	____× 8	____× 8	____× 8	____× 8
	____× 8	____× 8	____× 8	____× 8	____× 8
	____× 8 (60%)	____× 8 (65%)	____× 8	____× 6	____× 6
			____× 8 (70%)	____× 6 (72%)	____× 6 (72%)
Power clean	____× 6	____× 6	____× 6	____× 6	____× 6
	____× 5	____× 5	____× 5	____× 5	____× 5
	____× 5	____× 5	____× 5	____× 5	____× 5
	____× 5 (55%)	____× 5 (58%)	____× 5 (60%)	____× 4 (62%)	____× 4 (62%)
Behind-the-neck press	____× 10	____× 10	____× 10	____× 8	____× 8
	____× 8	____× 8	____× 8	____× 8	____× 8
	____× 8	____× 8	____× 8	____× 6	____× 6
	____× 8 (55%)	____× 8 (60%)	____× 8 (62%)	____× 6 (64%)	____× 6 (64%)
Bent-over rows	____× 10	____× 10	____× 10	____× 10	____× 10
	____× 10	____× 10	____× 10	____× 10	____× 10
Bicep curls	____× 10	____× 10	____× 10	____× 10	____× 10
	____× 10	____× 10	____× 10	____× 8	____× 8
Standing heel raises	____× 10	____× 10	____× 10	____× 10	____× 10
	____× 10	____× 10	____× 10	____× 10	____× 10
Neck resistance	____× 10	____× 10	____× 10	____× 10	____× 10
	____× 10	____× 10	____× 10	____× 8	____× 8
Sit-up crunch	____×____	____×____	____×____	____×____	____×____
	____×____	____×____	____×____	____×____	____×____
	____×____	____×____	____×____	____×____	____×____

Additional exercises:

In-Season
Mondays (continued)

Exercise	Week 6	Week 7	Week 8	Week 9	Week 10
Date:	_____	_____	_____	_____	_____
Back squat	____× 10	____× 10	____× 10	____× 10	____× 10
	____× 8	____× 8	____× 8	____× 8	____× 8
	____× 6	____× 6	____× 6	____× 6	____× 6
	____× 6 (52%)	____× 5 (54%)	____× 5 (54%)	____× 5 (56%)	____× 5 (56%)
Bench press	____× 10	____× 10	____× 10	____× 10	____× 10
	____× 8	____× 8	____× 8	____× 8	____× 8
	____× 8	____× 6	____× 6	____× 6	____× 6
	____× 6	____× 5	____× 5	____× 5	____× 5
	____× 6 (72%)	____× 5 (74%)	____× 5 (76%)	____× 5 (76%)	____× 4 (78%)
Power clean	____× 6	____× 6	____× 6	____× 6	____× 6
	____× 5	____× 5	____× 5	____× 5	____× 5
	____× 5	____× 5	____× 4	____× 4	____× 4
	____× 4 (64%)	____× 4 (64%)	____× 3 (66%)	____× 3 (66%)	____× 3 (68%)
Behind-the-neck press	____× 8	____× 8	____× 8	____× 8	____× 8
	____× 8	____× 6	____× 6	____× 6	____× 6
	____× 6	____× 5	____× 5	____× 5	____× 5
	____× 6 (64%)	____× 5 (66%)	____× 5 (66%)	____× 5 (66%)	____× 4 (68%)
Bent-over rows	____× 10	____× 8	____× 8	____× 8	____× 8
	____× 10	____× 8	____× 8	____× 8	____× 8
Bicep curls	____× 10	____× 8	____× 8	____× 8	____× 8
	____× 10	____× 8	____× 8	____× 8	____× 8
Standing heel raises	____× 10	____× 8	____× 8	____× 8	____× 8
	____× 10	____× 8	____× 8	____× 8	____× 8
Neck resistance	____× 10	____× 8	____× 8	____× 8	____× 8
	____× 10	____× 8	____× 8	____× 8	____× 8
Sit-up crunch	____×____	____×____	____×____	____×____	____×____
	____×____	____×____	____×____	____×____	____×____
	____×____	____×____	____×____	____×____	____×____

Additional exercises:

In-Season
Mondays (continued)

Date:	_____	_____	_____	_____
Exercise	**Week 11**	**Week 12**	**Week 13**	**Week 14**
Back squat	___× 8	___× 8	___× 8	___× 8
	___× 6	___× 6	___× 6	___× 6
	___× 5	___× 5	___× 5	___× 5
	___× 4 (58%)	___× 4 (58%)	___× 4 (60%)	___× 4 (60%)
Bench press	___× 10	___× 10	___× 10	___× 10
	___× 8	___× 8	___× 8	___× 8
	___× 6	___× 6	___× 6	___× 6
	___× 5	___× 5	___× 5	___× 5
	___× 4 (78%)	___× 4 (78%)	___× 3 (80%)	___× 3 (80%)
Power clean	___× 6	___× 6	___× 6	___× 6
	___× 5	___× 5	___× 5	___× 5
	___× 3	___× 3	___× 3	___× 3
	___× 2 (70%)	___× 2 (70%)	___× 2 (72%)	___× 2 (72%)
Behind-the-neck press	___× 8	___× 8	___× 8	___× 8
	___× 6	___× 6	___× 6	___× 6
	___× 5	___× 5	___× 5	___× 5
	___× 4 (68%)	___× 4 (68%)	___× 3 (70%)	___× 3 (70%)
Bent-over rows	___× 8	___× 8	___× 8	___× 8
	___× 8	___× 8	___× 8	___× 8
Bicep curls	___× 8	___× 8	___× 8	___× 8
	___× 8	___× 8	___× 8	___× 8
Standing heel raises	___× 8	___× 8	___× 8	___× 8
	___× 8	___× 8	___× 8	___× 8
Neck resistance	___× 8	___× 8	___× 8	___× 8
	___× 8	___× 8	___× 8	___× 8
Sit-up crunch	___×___	___×___	___×___	___×___
	___×___	___×___	___×___	___×___
	___×___	___×___	___×___	___×___

Additional exercises:

In-Season
Wednesdays

Date:	_____	_____	_____	_____	_____
Exercise	**Week 1**	**Week 2**	**Week 3**	**Week 4**	**Week 5**
Bench press	____× 10	____× 10	____× 10	____× 10	____× 10
	____× 8	____× 8	____× 8	____× 8	____× 8
	____× 8	____× 8	____× 8	____× 8	____× 8
	____× 8 (55%)	____× 8 (58%)	____× 8	____× 6	____× 6
			____× 8 (60%)	____× 6 (65%)	____× 6 (68%)
Leg press	____× 10	____× 10	____× 10	____× 10	____× 10
	____× 8	____× 8	____× 8	____× 8	____× 8
	____× 8	____× 8	____× 8	____× 6	____× 6
	____× 8 (45%)	____× 8 (48%)	____× 8 (50%)	____× 6 (52%)	____× 6 (52%)
Incline press	____× 10	____× 10	____× 10	____× 10	____× 8
	____× 8	____× 8	____× 8	____× 8	____× 8
	____× 8	____× 8	____× 8	____× 6	____× 6
	____× 8 (45%)	____× 8 (48%)	____× 8 (50%)	____× 6 (55%)	____× 6 (58%)
Shoulder shrugs	____× 10	____× 10	____× 10	____× 10	____× 10
	____× 10	____× 10	____× 10	____× 10	____× 10
Bent-over rows	____× 10	____× 10	____× 10	____× 10	____× 10
	____× 10	____× 10	____× 10	____× 10	____× 10
Bicep curls	____× 10	____× 10	____× 10	____× 10	____× 10
	____× 10	____× 10	____× 10	____× 10	____× 10
Leg curls	____× 10	____× 10	____× 10	____× 10	____× 10
	____× 10	____× 10	____× 10	____× 10	____× 10
Neck resistance	____× 10	____× 10	____× 10	____× 10	____× 10
	____× 10	____× 10	____× 10	____× 10	____× 10
Sit-up crunch	____×____	____×____	____×____	____×____	____×____
	____×____	____×____	____×____	____×____	____×____

Additional exercises:

Date:	_____	_____	_____	_____	_____
Exercise	**Week 6**	**Week 7**	**Week 8**	**Week 9**	**Week 10**
Bench press	___× 10	___× 10	___× 10	___× 10	___× 10
	___× 8	___× 8	___× 8	___× 8	___× 8
	___× 8	___× 6	___× 6	___× 6	___× 6
	___× 6	___× 5	___× 5	___× 5	___× 5
	___× 6 (68%)	___× 5 (70%)	___× 5 (70%)	___× 5 (70%)	___× 4 (72%)
Leg press	___× 10	___× 10	___× 10	___× 10	___× 10
	___× 8	___× 8	___× 8	___× 8	___× 8
	___× 6	___× 6	___× 6	___× 6	___× 6
	___× 6 (52%)	___× 5 (54%)	___× 5 (54%)	___× 5 (56%)	___× 5 (56%)
Incline press	___× 8	___× 8	___× 8	___× 8	___× 8
	___× 8	___× 6	___× 6	___× 6	___× 6
	___× 6	___× 5	___× 5	___× 5	___× 5
	___× 6 (58%)	___× 5 (60%)	___× 5 (60%)	___× 5 (60%)	___× 4 (62%)
Shoulder shrugs	___× 10	___× 8	___× 8	___× 8	___× 8
	___× 10	___× 8	___× 8	___× 8	___× 8
Bent-over rows	___× 10	___× 8	___× 8	___× 8	___× 8
	___× 10	___× 8	___× 8	___× 8	___× 8
Bicep curls	___× 10	___× 8	___× 8	___× 8	___× 8
	___× 10	___× 8	___× 8	___× 8	___× 8
Leg curls	___× 10	___× 8	___× 8	___× 8	___× 8
	___× 10	___× 8	___× 8	___× 8	___× 8
Neck resistance	___× 10	___× 8	___× 8	___× 8	___× 8
	___× 10	___× 8	___× 8	___× 8	___× 8
Sit-up crunch	___×___	___×___	___×___	___×___	___×___
	___×___	___×___	___×___	___×___	___×___

Additional exercises:

Exercise	Date: _____ Week 11	_____ Week 12	_____ Week 13	_____ Week 14
Bench press	____ × 10	____ × 10	____ × 10	____ × 10
	____ × 8	____ × 8	____ × 8	____ × 8
	____ × 6	____ × 6	____ × 6	____ × 6
	____ × 5	____ × 5	____ × 5	____ × 5
	____ × 4 (72%)	____ × 4 (72%)	____ × 3 (75%)	____ × 3 (75%)
Leg press	____ × 8	____ × 8	____ × 8	____ × 8
	____ × 6	____ × 6	____ × 6	____ × 6
	____ × 5	____ × 5	____ × 5	____ × 5
	____ × 4 (58%)	____ × 4 (58%)	____ × 4 (60%)	____ × 4 (60%)
Incline press	____ × 8	____ × 8	____ × 8	____ × 8
	____ × 6	____ × 6	____ × 6	____ × 6
	____ × 5	____ × 5	____ × 5	____ × 5
	____ × 4 (62%)	____ × 4 (62%)	____ × 4 (65%)	____ × 4 (65%)
Shoulder shrugs	____ × 8	____ × 8	____ × 8	____ × 8
	____ × 8	____ × 8	____ × 8	____ × 8
Bent-over rows	____ × 8	____ × 8	____ × 8	____ × 8
	____ × 8	____ × 8	____ × 8	____ × 8
Bicep curls	____ × 8	____ × 8	____ × 8	____ × 8
	____ × 8	____ × 8	____ × 8	____ × 8
Leg curls	____ × 8	____ × 8	____ × 8	____ × 8
	____ × 8	____ × 8	____ × 8	____ × 8
Neck resistance	____ × 8	____ × 8	____ × 8	____ × 8
	____ × 8	____ × 8	____ × 8	____ × 8
Sit-up crunch	____ × ____	____ × ____	____ × ____	____ × ____
	____ × ____	____ × ____	____ × ____	____ × ____

Additional exercises:

PART
III

STRENGTH-TRAINING EXERCISES

Core Exercises

Core exercises train the main muscles of the body (i.e., chest, shoulders, back, legs), which are important to the game of football. These exercises are also time-savers because one exercise trains several muscles at the same time. Perform these exercises to gain the total body strength you'll need for football.

BENCH PRESS

Ask any athlete how strong he is and he will tell you how much he can bench-press. Most athletes think the bench press is *the* measure of strength. In fact, the bench press is only a foundational exercise for developing and strengthening the upper body muscles (i.e., chest [pecs], shoulders [deltoids], and back of the arms [triceps]). It should always be combined with other upper body exercises and never used as the sole upper body developer.

The bench press is one of the most dangerous exercises because the weight is moved directly over the face and throat. You must be alert and concentrate fully on the exercise technique.

It is important to control the weight on the down phase to protect the rib cage and the fragile muscles and ligaments in that area. Never bounce the bar off your chest or use a towel to bounce it on. Touch the bar lightly to your chest and immediately begin the upward drive.

Spotting Technique

Always use a spotter. The spotter should stand behind the bar, close to your head. It's preferable for the spotter to be elevated because elevation provides leverage. The spotter's hands should be spaced evenly, very close to the bar, and should be able to grab the bar and pull the weight back up to the supports. The spotter can also provide a lift-off if it is needed. Usually only one spotter is needed; if you use heavy weights, however, you'll need three: one behind you and one on each side of the bar.

Breathing Technique

Unrack the bar, inhale, and hold your breath while lowering the bar. Then exhale *slowly* all the way to the top of the upward push. Or, if you prefer, unrack and position the bar first. Then inhale while lowering the bar and exhale slowly while pushing the bar up.

Exercise Technique

The bar is loaded evenly with collars.

Lie on the bench. Your eyes should be directly under the bar.

Place hands evenly on the bar, slightly wider than shoulder-width apart.

Wrap thumbs around the bar; lock wrists.

Rest your body and head on the bench throughout the exercise.

Spread legs to the sides of the bench.

Keep feet flat on floor, pointing slightly outward.

Lift the bar off the racks in a controlled manner.

Stabilize the bar over the upper part of the chest, keeping the arms straight, elbows locked, and grip tight (Figure 9.1a).

Pause.

Lower the bar slowly, maintaining control, to the chest close to the nipples (Figure 9.1, b and c).

Pause.

The elbow angle should be 90°.

Drive the bar up to the starting position (Figure 9.1, d and e).

Keep the head and hips on the bench.

Do not arch, twist the body, or move the feet.

Stay "tight-strong" throughout the movement (i.e., keep your muscles contracted, not limp).

Do not jam the bar at the top.

Return the bar to the rack in a controlled manner.

a

b

c

(continued)

Figure 9.1 Bench press.

d   e

Figure 9.1 *(continued)*

INCLINE PRESS

The incline press is great for strengthening the upper body, especially the shoulder area. It works the shoulder (deltoids), chest (pecs), back of arm (triceps) and upper back (trapezius) muscles. The hips and back are supported, which eliminates unnecessary stress on the lower back and enables you to lift more weight.

This exercise can be performed with various equipment, most commonly an Olympic bar with an incline bench. A preferred angle for the back rest of the incline bench is 40° to 45°. Many inclines are built at 35° or less. But at angles less than 35° the exercise is too similar to the bench press. By using a greater incline, you work your shoulders more.

Spotting Technique

Always use a spotter. For leverage, the spotter stands on a platform behind you. Most modern equipment has built-in spotter platforms. If no platform exists, the spotter should stand on a utility bench, close to you, with hands near the bar. If you cannot complete the upward movement, the spotter should quickly put his hands under the bar and pull the weight back up to the supports. As in the bench press, the spotter can also provide a lift-off if needed. Usually only one spotter is needed; if near-maximum weights are used, however, three are necessary, one behind you and one on each side.

Breathing Technique

Unrack the bar, inhale, and hold your breath while lowering the bar. Exhale *slowly* all the way to the top of the upward push. Or, if you prefer, unrack the bar and position first. Then inhale while lowering the bar and exhale slowly while pushing the bar up.

Exercise Technique

The bar is loaded evenly with collars.

Place hands evenly on the bar, slightly wider than shoulder-width apart.

Wrap thumbs around the bar; lock wrists.

Sit comfortably with hips and back secure on the bench, legs to the sides, feet flat on the floor, and head on the bench.

Take the bar off the supports slowly, in a controlled manner.

Stabilize the bar directly over your eyes (Figure 9.2a).

Pause.

Lower the bar, under control, to the top of the chest, close to the chin (Figure 9.2, b and c).

Keep the elbows out, forming a 90° angle.

The bar is lowered in an almost-straight line.

Pause.

Move the bar up in a straight line.

The arms are locked. Do not jam the bar (Figure 9.2, d and e).

Keep the body tight, the hips down, and the feet flat on the floor throughout the exercise.

Rack the bar securely on the support.

a   b   c

d   e

Figure 9.2 Incline press.

BEHIND-THE-NECK PRESS

The behind-the-neck press is the only major press in which you push the weight behind the head. This exercise helps strengthen the upper back muscles and provides a balance to the bench press. It also helps prevent rounded shoulders caused by excessive bench-press work. Specifically, it trains the shoulders (deltoids), arms (triceps), and upper back (trapezius). It also provides needed shoulder flexibility.

You can do the behind-the-neck press from either a standing or a seated position. The instructions given here assume a seated position, but the technique is the same regardless of the position. In the seated position, the upper back muscles are isolated. In the standing position, you might tend to use your legs to lift the weight. Because the weight is pushed over the head, you should wear a belt for lower back and abdominal stability in both the seated and standing positions.

Spotting Technique

Always use a spotter. For leverage, the spotter should stand in an elevated position behind the bar and close to your head. Usually only one spotter is needed; if heavy weights are used, however, three are necessary, one behind you and one on each side.

Breathing Technique

Unrack the bar, inhale, hold your breath while lowering the bar. Exhale *slowly* all the way to the top of the upward push. Or, if you prefer, unrack and position the bar first. Then inhale while lowering the bar and exhale slowly while pushing the bar up.

Exercise Technique

The bar is loaded evenly with collars and placed high on the upper back.

Place hands evenly on the bar and wrap thumbs around the bar.

Keep wrists straight and tight.

Elbows stay under bar, pointing out.

Sit with back straight, head up, and feet to the sides, flat on the floor (Figure 9.3a).

Push the bar up straight overhead (Figure 9.3, b and c).

Extend the arms to full length (Figure 9.3, d and e).

Do not jam the bar at the top.

Pause.

Lower the bar slowly, under control, to ear level (Figure 9.3f).

Pause.

Drive the bar upward again.

a   b   c   *(continued)*

Figure 9.3 Behind-the-neck press.

d   e   f

Figure 9.3 *(continued)*

BACK SQUAT

The back, or barbell, squat is often referred to as the *king of exercises*. I believe no other exercise trains the legs and hips as well. It should be performed with a full range of motion (down, parallel to the floor, and up to a vertical position) to provide optimum strength gains and to maintain or gain hip flexibility.

Because of the possibly high chance of injury, especially at the knee joint, some coaches think squatting is not worth the risk. Sufficient evidence exists indicating that the knee joint is actually strengthened through squatting. The exercise makes the muscles around the knee joint stronger. In my opinion, the squat is the most important lower body strength exercise for athletes.

The exercise trains the powerful, explosive muscles of the lower body (quadriceps, hamstrings, groin, hips, and lower back) used in running, jumping, and throwing. It is also a great time-saver because with this single exercise the athlete can strengthen the entire lower body.

You should use a safe apparatus such as a wide power rack with safety catch (squat inside rack) or a regular step rack with a safety bar at the bottom.

Some athletes cannot squat to a parallel position and keep their heels flat on the floor. This is usually the result of poor hip and ankle flexibility. Do not try to remedy the problem by putting a board or plates under your heels. This will do nothing to improve flexibility, and you will be doing the squat incorrectly. This "remedy" causes the body to shift forward and put too much pressure on the knees. Be patient; work on proper stance and flexibility by using light loads.

The use of chairs or boxes to squat on is also dangerous. Such equipment is usually used to teach sitting back and reaching proper depth. Never sit on a box or chair and relax when you have weight on your shoulders. This puts pressure on the lower back.

Spotting Technique

All squat workouts should be supervised by at least two spotters (one on each side of the bar). If the load is heavy, a third spotter should stand behind you. Spotters should never touch the bar unless you need help. Assistance is needed most often at the bottom position on the way up. If the spotters notice you are losing control or technique and cannot drive the bar up alone, they should automatically intervene by grabbing the bar and helping you rack it.

Breathing Technique

Inhale at the top of the squat, go down holding your breath, and exhale on the way up. You may find it easier to do most of the exhaling after passing the sticking point (halfway in the upward drive).

Exercise Technique

Place hands evenly on the bar, slightly wider than shoulder-width apart.

Rest the bar across the upper back and the back of the shoulders.

Keep the chest up and out, head up, shoulder blades together, and torso straight and tight.

Position feet shoulder-width apart or slightly wider.

Point toes slightly out; keep feet flat on the floor (Figure 9.4a).

Bend at the hips first (Figure 9.4b).

Then bend at the knees.

Bend knees and keep them over toes; do not move forward.

Sit back over heels (Figure 9.4c).

In a controlled manner, squat to where the upper leg is parallel to the floor.

Pause. Do not bounce (Figure 9.4d).

Drive up to the starting position, maintaining control (Figure 9.4e).

Keep hips under the bar and feet flat.

Keep knees out, chest up, shoulders back, and head up.

Keep the weight centered in the upward drive.

Don't jam the bar at the top (Figure 9.4f).

a   b   c   *(continued)*

Figure 9.4 Back squat.

d

e

f

Figure 9.4 *(continued)*

LEG PRESS

The leg press is an excellent exercise for strengthening the lower body. Its simplicity also allows you to use relatively heavy weights. It is one of the safer exercises because the weight is supported by the machine.

The leg press develops the lower body by extending the knees and hips. It works the quadriceps, hamstrings, hips, and groin. The hip angle used in the leg press dictates how much work the hips and upper part of the hamstrings get. If the angle is tighter (knees close to the chest), you have to give a longer push, working groin muscles and upper hamstrings harder.

The leg press is popular because it can be performed with a variety of machines. Depending on the equipment you are using, you may be seated, lying back on the floor, or pronated at a variety of angles.

Spotting Technique

Spotters are not generally used in this exercise.

Breathing Technique

Inhale at the bottom or while the weight is lowered, and exhale while driving the weight upward. Do not hold your breath while performing several repetitions; inhale and exhale for each repetition.

Sometimes an athlete gets a headache or blacks out while doing this exercise. This is due to improper breathing technique. If this happens to you, you are holding your breath for too long.

Exercise Technique

Lie on your back.

Keep the back and head down on the support.

Place feet on the leg press, approximately shoulder-width apart.

Point toes slightly outward.

The pressure should be on the ball and heel of the foot.

The hip angle is approximately 45°.

The hips are flat against the bench.

Place hands to the sides for stability (Figure 9.5a).

Press with force toward the top.

Point the knees out in push (Figure 9.5b).

The head stays down and is relaxed.

Extend the legs fully, but do not lock the knees (Figure 9.5c).

Do not jam the weight at the top.

Pause.

Lower the weight slowly back to the starting position.

Do not bounce at the bottom.

Pause and repeat.

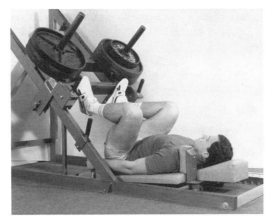
a

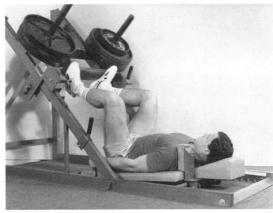
b

c

Figure 9.5 Leg press.

DEAD LIFT

The dead lift is one of the best tests of overall body strength. It is often associated with power lifting. The competitive power lifter tries to lift as much as possible. This can give you the wrong impression. The dead lift should be used as a training exercise, not as a competition. Like any other exercise, proper technique and intensity must be used.

The dead lift is a multijoint exercise involving the knees, hips, back, and to some degree the shoulders. This exercise trains all the muscles of the lower body: the quadriceps, hamstrings, groin, hip flexors, gluteus maximus, lower back erectors, and to a degree the trapezius and latissimus dorsi in the upper back. These are the same muscles used in sports that require thrusting of the hips and movements such as blocking, tackling, jumping, running, and throwing.

Spotting Technique

Spotters are not generally used in this exercise.

Breathing Technique

Inhale at the bottom when in the pulling stance. Hold your breath during the entire pull to the top. Then slowly exhale while lowering the bar to the starting position.

Exercise Technique

Stand with feet flat on floor, shoulder-width apart, toes pointing slightly out, and bar touching shins.

Place hands outside legs, slightly wider than shoulder-width apart.

Grab the bar with one palm facing in, one palm facing out, thumbs wrapped around bar.

Assume the correct posture: Arms straight, elbows slightly touching legs; head up; chest up and out; back straight; shoulders back; hips low, below shoulders; and thighs parallel to the floor (Figure 9.6, a and b).

Lift the bar slowly (Figure 9.6c).

Pull by extending legs and hips.

Keep the arms straight and the back straight.

Keep the bar close to the body when pulling.

Pull evenly to a standing position (Figure 9.6, d and e).

The head faces forward.

Keep the shoulders in line with the body.

Do not lean back (Figure 9.6f).

Pause.

Lower the weight slowly

Bend at the hips and knees.

Keep the bar close to the body.

Keep the arms straight.

a

b

c

d

e

f

Figure 9.6 Dead lift.

WALKING LUNGE

Most lower body exercises work both legs simultaneously, but lunges require you to work one leg at a time. Because of this, lunges stretch and strengthen certain hip and groin muscles as no other exercise can. It also trains the ankles slightly. The walking lunge works the same muscles as the back squat and leg press do but places more emphasis on the groin and top of the hamstring.

It is advantageous to strength-train one leg at a time because many movements require the legs to move one at a time. Improving the individual strength of the legs can help you run faster and jump higher.

Spotting Technique

This exercise requires two spotters, one on each side of the bar. They will move along with you as you do the walking lunges. Their role is to grab the bar or assist if you are off balance.

Breathing Technique

Breathe normally throughout the exercise. Inhale as you step and lower the body. Exhale as you drive up the front leg.

Exercise Technique

The bar is loaded evenly with collars.

The bar is placed high on the upper back across the trapezius muscles and the shoulders.

Hold the bar comfortably with hands to the sides.

Stand straight, feet shoulder-width apart (Figure 9.7a).

Step forward with dominant leg, heel first (Figure 9.7, b-d).

Take a long but comfortable step.

Lower the body until forward thigh is parallel to floor.

The back leg remains almost straight.

Your weight is on the toes of the back foot.

The front foot is flat on the ground.

The front knee is directly over the toes.

Keep the upper body straight, the head up, and the chest up and out (Figure 9.7e).

Pause. Do not bounce.

Push off with the front leg up to a standing position (Figure 9.7f). Maintain control of movement.

The upper body stays erect.

Repeat with the opposite leg (Figure 9.7, g-k).

a   b   c   *(continued)*

Figure 9.7 Walking lunge.

Figure 9.7   *(continued)*

HIGH PULL

The high pull, the easiest of all explosive pulling exercises, is the core of all pulling movements. If you have not mastered the high pull, do not move on to the power clean.

The high pull works the legs, hips, lower back, upper back, and shoulders simultaneously. The calves and ankles are also worked when you stand on your toes. As you extend your knees, the hamstrings and quadriceps are worked. Because of the hip drive, the muscles of the lower back and entire hip area are strengthened. The upper back muscles (latissimus dorsi, trapezius) are worked when the weight is shrugged and pulled up. The shoulders and biceps get some work when you pull with your arms and bring the bar close to your chin.

The high pull is more than a strength builder. Because it is performed quickly and explosively, it trains the working muscles to be more powerful. It develops power in the lower body, which makes you a faster, more explosive athlete.

Spotting Technique

Spotters are not generally used in this exercise.

Breathing Technique

Inhale at the bottom in the pulling stance, and hold your breath during the entire pull to the top. Slowly exhale while lowering the bar to the starting position.

Exercise Technique

Stand with feet shoulder-width apart.

Point toes out slightly.

The feet are flat on floor.

The bar touches the shins.

Grab bar using overhand grip, and wrap thumbs around the bar.

Space hands evenly, slightly wider than shoulder-width apart.

Assume correct posture: arms locked, back straight, face forward; hips parallel to knees; shoulders high and back, chest out; and upper body over the bar (Figure 9.8a).

Ease the bar off floor slowly by extending the legs (Figure 9.8b).

Do not pull with the arms.

Bring the bar up straight (not around legs), keeping the bar close to the body.

The bar passes the knees into the power position (Figure 9.8c).

The back and arms remain straight, head up.

Now, pull the bar explosively by extending the legs and hips and shrugging with the shoulders (Figure 9.8d).

Extend the body fully up on the toes.

Pull the bar close to the body.

Now, continue the upward pull by pulling with the arms (Figure 9.8e).

Keep the elbows high and out.

Pull the bar to nipple height (Figure 9.8f).

Pause.

Lower the bar, under control, by bending at the hips and knees.

a   b   c

d   e   f

Figure 9.8 High pull.

POWER CLEAN

This total-body exercise trains the legs, hips, lower back, upper back, and shoulders (as does the high pull). The calves and ankles are worked when you stand on your toes; when you extend your knees, the hamstrings and quadriceps are worked. Because of hip rotation, the muscles of the lower back and entire hip area (gluteus maximus and hip muscles) are also strengthened. The upper back muscles (latissimus dorsi, trapezius) are worked when the weight is pulled up in shrugging. The shoulders and biceps get some work when the bar is pulled with the arms. There is even some shoulder girdle development when the bar is racked and the elbows brought forward. Like the high pull, the power clean is done quickly and explosively. It has been proved that pulling movements, such as those in the power clean, produce maximum human power during the execution.

Spotting Technique

Spotters are not generally used in this exercise.

Breathing Technique

Inhale at the bottom when in the pulling stance, and hold your breath during the entire pull to the top. Slowly exhale while lowering the bar to the starting position.

Exercise Technique

Stand with feet shoulder-width apart, toes pointing out slightly, feet flat on the floor, and bar touching the shins.

Grab the bar with an overhand grip, thumbs wrapped around bar.

Assume the correct posture: Back straight, shoulders back, arms straight; head up facing forward; hips parallel to the knees; and upper body over the bar (Figure 9.9, a and b).

Ease the bar off the floor slowly by extending the legs.

Bring the bar up straight (not around legs). (See Figure 9.10, a-d.)

Keep the bar close to body (Figure 9.9c).

Move the knees back under the bar into the power position (Figure 9.9d).

Pull the bar explosively by extending the legs and hips (Figure 9.9e).

Extend the body and stand on the toes.

Shrug the shoulders to elevate the bar (Figure 9.9f).

Continue upward pull by pulling with arms (Figure 9.9, g and h).

When bar reaches the highest point, move the body under the bar.

Spread feet slightly to the sides.

Bend at the knees.

Rack the weight across the top of the shoulders (Figure 9.9i).

Point elbows out and high.

Stand up with the bar on the shoulders.

Lower the bar under control to the top of the thighs.

Then bend at the knees and hips; squatting down, bring the bar to the floor.

a

b

(continued)

Figure 9.9 Power clean.

c

d

e

f

g

Figure 9.9   *(continued)*

h   i

Figure 9.9 *(continued)*

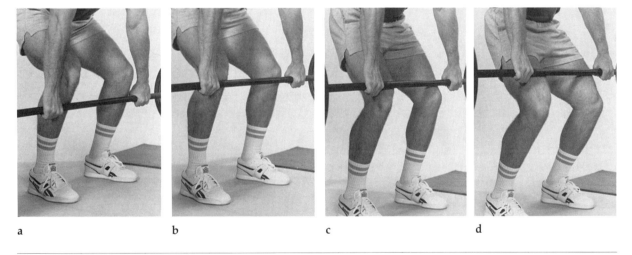

a   b   c   d

Figure 9.10 Movement of the bar along the legs.

CHAPTER
10

Auxiliary Exercises

All workouts need to be supplemented with a variety of auxiliary exercises, which can be used to isolate and strengthen specific areas and can provide sport-specific strength training. The combination of core and auxiliary exercises will ensure that all muscle areas are strength-trained. You will not necessarily need a spotter for the auxiliary exercises.

NECK MANUAL RESISTANCE EXERCISES

Because neck strength is very important to football players, you will do neck exercises extensively, whereas other athletes, like tennis players or golfers, do not.

A strong neck is necessary to help reduce the chance of injury when contact is made with the upper body. The power clean, high pull, and shrug movements work the trapezius muscle, which is important in strengthening the neck. But the neck also needs to be strengthened in its four moving planes: *Neck flexion* moves the head forward toward the chest; *neck extension* pushes the head back toward the shoulders; *right lateral flexion* moves the right ear toward the right shoulder; and *left lateral flexion* moves the left ear toward the left shoulder.

When no machines are available, a partner can apply the resistance. It is critical that your partner know you well and understand how much resistance is needed. Partners must communicate and work together for the best results.

Breathing Technique

Exhale when flexing the neck, inhale when returning to starting position.

Exercise Technique

Lie on a bench with torso stable and head hanging off the end.

Your partner stands near you, using a towel for comfort and stability, and adds resistance.

The resistance is gradual and constant, increasing as repetitions progress; very little resistance is applied in the first few reps.

Take 4 or 5 seconds to execute full range of motion.

Stop momentarily when action is finished and return to starting position.

A. Lie on your back. Your partner places resistance on your forehead while you push up toward your chest (Figure 10.1, a-d).

B. Lie on your stomach. Your partner puts resistance on the back of your head as you push up toward your shoulders (Figure 10.2, a-c).

C. Lie on your back. Your partner puts resistance on the right side of your head while you push toward your right shoulder (Figure 10.3, a and b).

D. Continue lying on your back. Your partner puts resistance on the left side of your head while you push toward your left shoulder (Figure 10.4, a-c).

One rep is completing the exercise on all four sides.

a

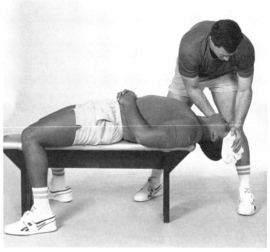

b

c

d

Figure 10.1 Neck flexion with manual resistance.

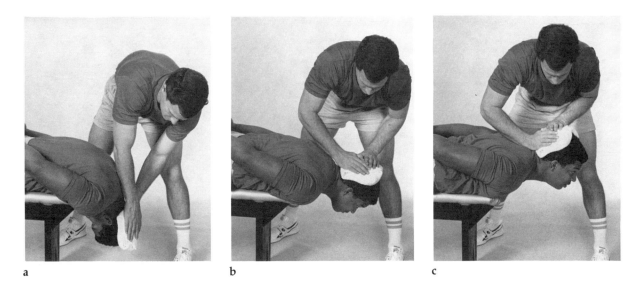

a   b   c

Figure 10.2 Neck extension with manual resistance.

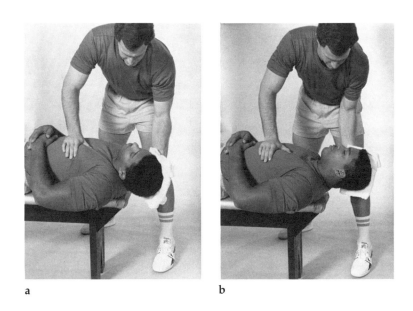

a   b

Figure 10.3 Right lateral flexion with manual resistance.

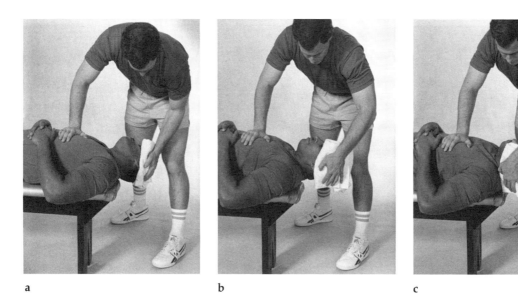

a   b   c

Figure 10.4 Left lateral flexion with manual resistance.

NECK VARIABLE RESISTANCE MACHINE EXERCISES

All neck-strengthening machines do basically the same thing. Movements must be done slowly and under control. Resistance machines exercise the neck muscles just as manual resistance does.

Breathing Technique

Exhale when flexing the neck, inhale when returning to starting position.

Exercise Technique

Sit comfortably, and grab the handles of the machine for torso stability (Figure 10.5a).

The head pads should be placed to allow free movement in a full range of motion.

Torso and shoulders do not move.

Don't make any forcing, jamming, or explosive movements.

Exert force against the pad in a full range of motion on all four sides (Front, back, right side, left side), as in manual resistance exercises (Figure 10.5, b-i).

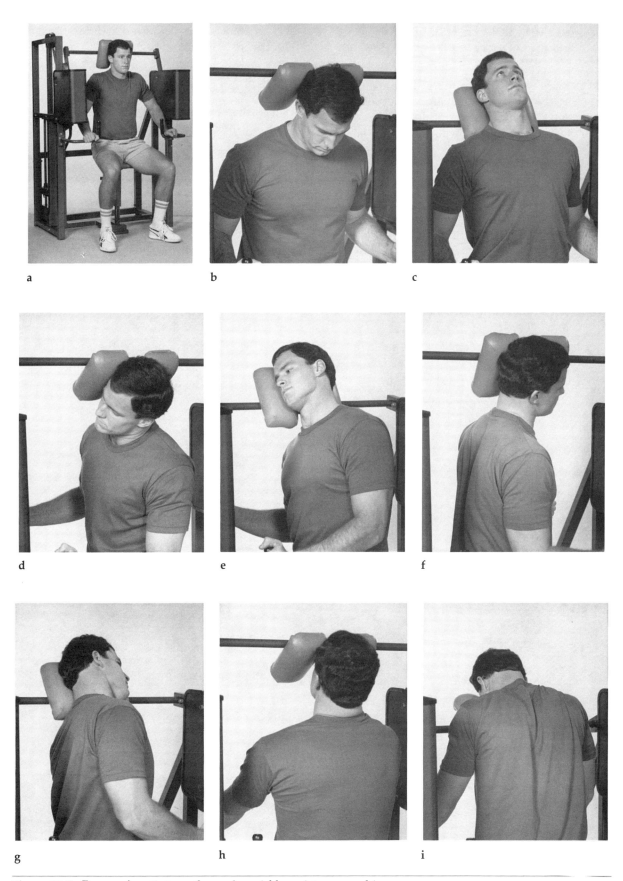

Figure 10.5 Range of motion on the neck variable resistance machine.

ALTERNATE INCLINE DUMBBELL PRESSES

This exercise works primarily the deltoid muscles in the shoulder. The deltoids are a group of three specific muscles: the anterior, middle, and posterior deltoids. To properly train all parts of the shoulder, resistance must be moved in different planes. The triceps and upper back are also trained.

Breathing Technique

Exhale when extending the dumbbell, inhale when lowering the dumbbell back to the shoulder.

Exercise Technique

Sit on an incline utility bench or an incline bench press with an angle of 35° to 45°.

Rest back and head on the bench.

Place legs to the sides and feet flat on the floor.

Hold a dumbbell in each hand and rest hands close to the shoulders.

Elbows should be out and to the sides in line with the shoulders (Figure 10.6a).

While keeping the left dumbbell down, push the right dumbbell up in complete extension straight over your face (Figure 10.6b).

Pause.

Lower to shoulder under control (Figure 10.6c).

Repeat same movement with the left side (Figure 10.6, d and e).

Do not lift shoulders or head off the bench.

As a variation you may push both dumbbells up and down at the same time.

a   b   c   *(continued)*

Figure 10.6 Alternate incline dumbbell presses.

d   e

Figure 10.6   *(continued)*

DUMBBELL FLYS

For maximum development of the chest, workouts can be supplemented with very specific chest exercises. The dumbbell flys exercise is designed to develop the chest and improve strength.

Breathing Technique

Exhale when raising the dumbbells, inhale when lowering the dumbbells.

Exercise Technique

Lie on a flat utility bench with the head resting on the bench.

Place legs to the sides and feet flat on the floor.

The palms of the hands are facing each other.

The dumbbells are extended overhead (Figure 10.7a).

Bending the elbow slightly, lower the dumbbells in line with the shoulder (Figure 10.7b).

Keep the elbows pointed down and back.

The shoulder, elbow, and dumbbell should form a straight line in the up-and-down movement.

Lower the dumbbells as far as flexibility permits (Figure 10.7c).

Pause at the bottom.

Slowly bring the dumbbells back to the starting position.

At the top touch the dumbbells together slightly.

The head or shoulders should never come off the bench.

Concentrate on contracting the chest muscles when pulling the dumbbells upward.

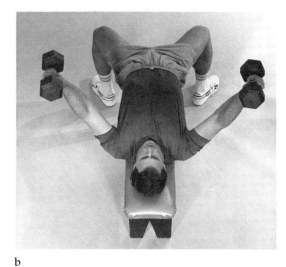

a   b

c

Figure 10.7   Dumbbell flys.

BICEP CURLS

Even though the arms may not be a major area in sport performance, arm workouts are important for total body strength. Most athletes dream of having big arms, big triceps, and big biceps. This exercise will help strengthen your biceps.

Breathing Technique

Exhale when raising the bar, inhale when lowering the bar.

Exercise Technique

Stand with feet shoulder-width apart, body erect.

Grab the bar (straight or curl) with hands about shoulder-width apart, palms facing up.

Hold your arms straight with the bar resting in front, close to the legs (Figure 10.8a).

Curl the bar upward all the way to the chin (Figure 10.8, b and c).

Keep elbows close to the body.

Pause at the top position.

Slowly lower the bar back to the starting position.

There should be no hip or back movement.

This exercise can also be done with dumbbells.

a   b   c

Figure 10.8 Bicep curls.

TRICEP EXTENSIONS

This exercise will strengthen the triceps muscle in your arms. When performing this exercise, be careful not to bounce the bar at the bottom or open your elbows out to the side in the upward movement.

Breathing Technique

Exhale when extending the arm, inhale when returning to the starting position.

Exercise Technique

Lie on a bench; place feet to the sides.

Hold the bar with hands slightly less than shoulder-width apart.

Raise the bar overhead at arm's length straight over your face (Figure 10.9a).

By bending at the elbows, slowly lower the bar backward toward your forehead (Figure 10.9b).

Hold the upper arms close to the head.

Keep elbows close together.

Lower the bar to 90° (Figure 10.9c).

Pause.

Bring the bar back to the starting position.

a   b   c

Figure 10.9 Tricep extensions.

DIPS

This exercise is great for training the triceps, but it also works the shoulders. If you do not wish to train the shoulders, you should choose another tricep exercise. To add resistance, weight can be tied around your waist with a special belt.

Breathing Technique

Exhale when extending the arms, inhale when returning to the starting position.

Exercise Technique

Keeping the body straight and the arms locked, support your weight on the dip bar (Figure 10.10a).

Your grip is slightly wider than shoulder-width apart.

For more comfort, you can bend the knees and cross the right foot over the left.

Lower your body to the point where the upper arm is parallel to the floor (Figure 10.10, b and c).

Pause.

Raise your body back up to the starting position (arms fully extended).

At the top, stop momentarily. Repeat the movement.

During the upward drive the body should not swing or twist.

a   b   c

Figure 10.10 Dips.

WRIST CURLS

Hand and forearm strength are especially important in football, where hands are used extensively. Many athletes, however, neglect an important part of arm strength—wrist strength. Wrist curls should be performed at a moderate speed, under control. This exercise can also be performed seated, with the forearms resting on the quads, and it can be done with dumbbells.

Breathing Technique

Exhale when raising the weight, inhale when lowering the weight.

Exercise Technique

Kneel at the side of a flat utility bench.

Grab the bar with hands about 6 inches apart.

The forearms and elbows are placed flat on the bench for support and stability.

The hands and bar hang off the side of the bench (Figure 10.11a).

Lower the bar to the starting position.

At the bottom position, the bar can be allowed to roll to the tip of the fingers for more wrist flexion (Figure 10.11b). Roll it back into the hand before the upward pull.

Curl the bar up as far as possible using only the wrist (Figure 10.11c).

Stop momentarily.

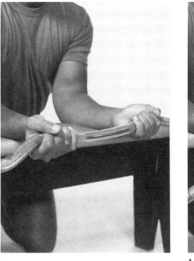  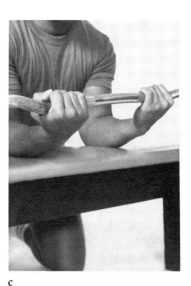

a   b   c

Figure 10.11 Wrist curls.

BENT-OVER ROWS

Most athletes are interested in developing the front of the upper body and neglect its counterpart, the upper back. This is a very large, strong area that includes the trapezius, rhomboids, and latissimus dorsi as its main muscle groups. Upper back strength is important in sports (such as football) that require pulling movements. Football players often have superior upper back strength compared to other athletes.

Breathing Technique

Exhale when bringing the bar to the chest, inhale when lowering the bar.

Exercise Technique

Stand with feet shoulder-width apart.

Grab the bar with palms down, shoulder-width apart (Figure 10.12a).

Bend at the knees and lower the hips back as the upper back is bent forward to a position almost parallel to the floor (Figure 10.12, b and c).

Arms are straight, holding the bar close to the body.

Shoulders are back.

Keep the head up, looking forward, and the torso tight.

Keeping the elbows close to the body, slowly pull the weight to the abdomen (Figure 10.12d).

Pause.

Lower the bar slowly to the starting position.

a

b

c

d

Figure 10.12   Bent-over rows.

SHOULDER SHRUGS

This exercise, like the bent-over rows, works the upper back. All of the work should be done with the trapezius muscles.

Breathing Technique

Exhale when lifting the shoulders, inhale when lowering the shoulders.

Exercise Technique

Stand erect with feet shoulder-width apart.

Hold the bar close to the body with arms straight, palms down, and hands about shoulder-width apart (Figure 10.13a).

Raise the weight by shrugging the shoulders toward the ears (Figure 10.13b).

Lean forward slightly.

Keep the head and body still while elevating the shoulders as high as possible in a straight upward line (Figure 10.13c).

The shoulders should not rotate.

Hold the weight momentarily at the top.

Slowly lower it back to the starting position.

a   b   c

Figure 10.13 Shoulder shrugs.

BACK RAISES

Only a few core exercises—dead lift, power clean, high pull, and back squat—train the lower back. Often this area is overlooked and untrained. Back raises are meant to supplement these exercises.

The main muscles worked in the lower back are the spinal erectors.

Breathing Technique

Exhale when raising the upper body, inhale when lowering the upper body to starting position.

Exercise Technique

Lie facedown on the equipment.

The pad should be under your thighs to permit free movement of the hips and lower back.

The feet are securely supported under the foot holders.

The back is straight, shoulders back, chest out, and head in line with the torso.

The arms are crossed on the chest or behind the head (Figure 10.14a).

Bend at the hips and lower your torso until it is perpendicular to the floor (Figure 10.14b).

Maintain a tight, strong upper and lower back.

Pause.

Using lower back muscles, slowly raise the torso back to the starting position (Figure 10.14, c and d).

Do not hyperextend, twist, or bounce at the bottom to gain momentum.

Perform this exercise at moderate speed, under control.

For the more advanced athlete with good lower back strength, a weight plate can be held for added resistance.

a

b

c

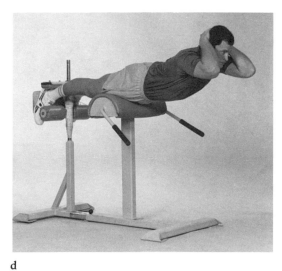
d

Figure 10.14 Back raises.

SIT-UP CRUNCH

All sports require abdominal strength for stability, bending, pulling, and twisting. Sometimes abdominal strength is confused with hip-flexor strength because the hip flexors are tied in very close in that area. Abdominal strength is usually inferior to hip-flexor strength; therefore, for mus-cular balance the abdominals need to be strengthened independently. To strengthen this area, you need to do exercises that bend the trunk forward and side to side.

Breathing Technique

Inhale on the way up, exhale on the way down.

Exercise Technique

Lie on your back with knees bent and feet flat on floor close to buttocks, arms crossed behind the head (Figure 10.15a).

For added resistance, a weight can be held on the chest.

Curl at the shoulders first (Figure 10.15b).

Than curl at the upper back, and then the lower back (Figure 10.15c).

You do not need to curl all the way to the knees.

Pause at the top.

Keep the knees up.

Lower the back to the floor.

The lower back touches the floor first.

Do not jerk or twist.

Do not relax at the bottom.

Keep the abdominals tight and the shoulders curled inward.

a

b

c

Figure 10.15 Sit-up crunch.

OBLIQUE TWISTS

In addition to abdominal strength, football also requires oblique strength for stability, bending, pulling, and twisting. Obliques are the side muscles in the body's midsection. This exercise, however, is not for beginner athletes because it requires good abdominal and lower back strength.

Breathing Technique

Exhale when twisting upward, inhale when twisting downward to the starting position.

Exercise Technique

Sit on the machine with feet under the foot supports.

The torso hangs off the apparatus.

Put your hands together and extend your arms straight over your face (Figure 10.16a).

Twist the torso to the right (Figure 10.16b).

Keep hips flat on the pad.

Return to the straight position (Figure 10.16c).

Twist to the left (Figure 10.16d).

Twisting to both sides and back to the start position is one repetition.

For added resistance, the advanced athlete may hold dumbbells or weight plates, as shown in Figure 10.16a-d.

a

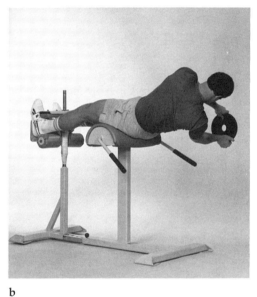
b

c

d

Figure 10.16   Oblique twists.

LEG EXTENSIONS

When we refer to leg strength, we almost always think of the quadriceps muscle in the front of the leg. Leg extensions will strengthen this muscle. While you perform this exercise, keep the trunk straight at all times so the quads do the work. The hips and torso should not move or swing to help bring the weight up.

Breathing Technique

Exhale when raising the weight, inhale when lowering the weight.

Exercise Technique

Sit on the machine, hands holding on to the sides for stability.

Place feet under the moving pads.

The knee joint should be slightly off the pad.

The bottom roller should be on the lower part of the shin close to the feet (Figure 10.17a).

Fully extend the legs straight forward (Figure 10.17, b and c).

Pause.

Gradually lower the weight to the starting position.

Do not lower all the way; keep some tension.

The upward movement should be quicker than the lowering but still controlled.

The trunk should be kept straight at all times.

a   b   c

Figure 10.17   Leg extensions.

LEG CURLS

The back part of the leg, the hamstring, is important to leg strength, just as the quadriceps is. Leg curls strengthen the hamstrings. Many hamstring injuries occur because athletes have not put enough emphasis on strengthening this muscle and too much emphasis on the quadriceps.

Breathing Technique

Exhale when raising the weight, inhale when lowering the weight.

Exercise Technique

Lie facedown on the machine, body straight, hands holding on to the side of the machine for stability.

The head faces forward and the knees rest off the pad.

The feet are under the pad with the pad resting on the Achilles tendon area (Figure 10.18a).

Curl the weight up by flexing at the knees (Figure 10.18, b and c).

The hips must stay flat on the machine.

Pause at the top.

Slowly bring the weight down to the starting position.

At the bottom, the legs do not relax but keep some tension.

Do not bounce the weight at the bottom.

The torso should remain still; the only movement is at the knees.

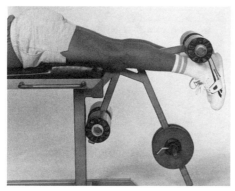
a

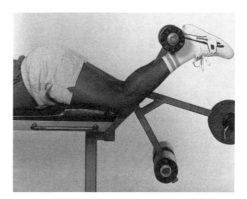
b

c

Figure 10.18 Leg curls.

STANDING HEEL RAISES

Seldom referred to, but almost as important as quadriceps and hamstring strength, is ankle and calf strength. Standing heel raises work the calf muscles, which extend from the ankle to the knee. Also trained are the Achilles tendons, helping them to be more flexible and to move in a full range of motion. This exercise also works all the muscles and tendons around the ankle, giving strength and flexibility in that area.

Breathing Technique

Exhale when rising on the toes, inhale when lower the body to starting position.

Exercise Technique

The bar should rest high on the shoulders.

The hands hold the bar with the elbows pointing down.

The head looks up and the body is straight.

Step up on the wood block.

All of your weight is supported on the toes and balls of the feet (Figure 10.19a).

The feet should be 8 to 12 inches apart, pointing straight forward (Figure 10.19b).

In this position extend straight up as high as possible, keeping the legs straight (Figure 10.19c).

Pause at top; then slowly lower the heels lower than the block (Figure 10.19, d and e).

The exercise can also be performed standing and seated with a variety of machines.

a

b

c

d

e

Figure 10.19 Standing heel raises.

APPENDIX A

Strength-Training Percentages Table

Weight(lb)	40%	45%	50%	55%	60%	65%	70%	75%	80%	85%	90%	95%
100	40	45	50	55	60	65	70	75	80	85	90	95
110	45	50	55	60	65	70	75	85	90	95	100	105
120	50	55	60	65	70	80	85	90	95	100	110	115
130	55	60	65	70	80	85	90	100	105	110	115	125
140	55	65	70	75	85	90	100	105	110	120	125	135
150	60	70	75	85	90	100	105	115	120	130	135	145
160	65	75	80	90	95	105	110	120	130	135	145	150
170	70	80	85	95	100	110	120	125	135	145	155	160
180	70	80	90	100	110	115	125	135	145	155	160	170
190	75	85	90	105	115	125	135	145	150	160	170	180
200	80	90	100	110	120	130	140	150	160	170	180	190
210	85	100	105	115	125	135	145	155	170	180	190	200
220	90	100	110	120	130	145	155	165	175	185	200	210
230	95	105	115	125	140	150	160	175	185	195	205	220
240	95	110	120	130	145	155	170	180	190	205	215	230
250	100	115	125	140	150	165	175	190	200	215	225	240
260	105	120	130	145	155	170	180	195	210	220	235	245
270	110	125	135	150	160	175	190	200	215	230	245	255
280	110	125	140	155	170	180	195	210	225	240	250	265
290	115	130	145	160	175	190	205	220	230	245	260	275
300	120	135	150	165	180	195	210	225	240	255	270	285
310	125	140	155	170	185	200	215	230	250	265	280	295
320	130	145	160	175	190	210	225	240	255	270	290	305
330	135	150	165	180	200	215	230	250	265	280	300	315
340	135	155	170	190	205	220	240	255	270	290	305	325
350	140	160	175	195	210	230	245	265	280	300	315	335
360	145	160	180	200	220	230	250	270	290	310	320	340
370	150	170	185	205	220	240	260	280	295	315	330	350
380	150	170	190	210	230	250	265	285	305	325	340	360
390	160	180	200	210	230	250	270	290	310	330	350	370
400	160	180	200	220	240	260	280	300	320	340	360	380

(continued)

Weight(lb)	40%	45%	50%	55%	60%	65%	70%	75%	80%	85%	90%	95%
410	165	185	205	225	245	265	285	310	330	350	370	390
420	170	190	210	230	250	270	290	320	340	360	380	400
430	170	195	215	235	260	280	300	320	345	365	390	410
440	175	200	220	240	265	285	310	330	350	375	395	420
450	180	200	230	250	270	290	320	340	360	380	410	430
460	185	210	230	250	275	300	320	345	370	390	415	440
470	190	210	235	260	280	305	330	350	375	400	425	445
480	190	220	240	260	290	310	340	360	380	410	430	460
490	195	220	245	270	295	320	345	370	395	415	440	465
500	200	225	250	275	300	325	350	375	400	425	450	475
510	200	230	260	280	310	330	360	380	410	430	460	490
520	210	235	260	285	315	340	365	390	415	440	470	495
530	210	240	265	290	320	345	370	400	425	450	480	505
540	220	240	270	300	320	350	380	410	430	460	490	510
550	220	250	275	300	330	360	385	410	440	465	495	520
560	225	250	280	310	335	365	390	420	450	475	505	530
570	230	260	290	310	340	370	400	430	460	480	510	540
580	230	260	290	320	350	375	405	435	465	490	520	550
590	235	265	295	325	355	385	415	440	470	500	530	560
600	240	270	300	330	360	390	420	450	480	510	540	570

Note: Percentage weights are rounded to nearest 5 lb.

APPENDIX B

Core Exercise
Weight Progression Chart

Set 1	Set 2	Set 3	Set 4	Set 5	Set 6
75	85	95	105	115	125
75	85	95	110	120	130
75	90	105	115	125	135
75	90	105	120	130	140
85	95	110	125	135	145
85	95	110	130	140	150
85	105	115	135	145	155
85	105	115	135	150	160
95	110	125	140	155	165
95	110	125	140	155	170
95	115	130	145	160	175
95	115	130	150	165	180
95	125	140	155	170	185
95	125	140	160	175	190
95	135	150	165	180	195
95	135	150	170	185	200
135	145	160	175	190	205
135	145	160	180	195	210
135	155	170	185	200	215
135	155	170	190	205	220
135	155	180	195	210	225
135	155	180	200	215	230
135	155	185	200	215	235
135	155	185	205	220	240
135	155	185	205	225	245
135	155	185	210	230	250
135	155	185	215	235	255
135	155	185	220	240	260
135	155	185	225	245	265
135	155	185	230	250	270
135	155	195	235	255	275

(continued)

Set 1	Set 2	Set 3	Set 4	Set 5	Set 6
135	155	195	240	260	280
135	185	225	245	265	285
135	185	225	250	270	290
135	185	225	255	275	295
135	185	225	260	280	300
135	185	225	265	285	305
135	185	225	270	290	310
135	185	225	275	295	315
135	185	225	280	300	320
135	185	245	285	305	325
135	185	245	290	310	330
135	225	255	295	315	335
135	225	255	300	320	340
135	225	255	305	325	345
135	225	255	310	330	350
135	225	275	315	335	355
135	225	275	320	340	360
135	225	275	325	345	365
135	225	275	325	350	370
135	225	275	330	355	375
135	225	275	335	360	380
135	225	275	335	365	385
135	225	275	340	370	390
135	225	315	345	375	395
135	225	315	350	380	400
135	225	315	355	385	405
135	225	315	360	390	410
135	225	315	365	395	415
135	225	315	370	400	420
135	225	315	375	405	425
135	225	315	380	410	430
135	225	315	380	415	435
135	225	315	385	415	440
135	225	315	385	415	445
135	225	315	390	420	450
135	225	315	390	420	455
135	225	315	395	430	460
135	225	315	400	435	465
135	225	315	405	440	470
135	225	315	405	445	475
135	225	315	415	450	480
225	315	365	425	455	485
225	315	365	430	460	490
225	315	365	435	465	495
225	315	365	440	470	500
225	315	365	445	475	505
225	315	365	450	480	510
225	315	405	455	485	515
225	315	405	460	490	520
225	315	405	465	495	525
225	315	405	465	500	530
225	315	405	465	505	535
225	315	405	470	510	540
225	315	405	475	515	545
225	315	405	480	520	550

Set 1	Set 2	Set 3	Set 4	Set 5	Set 6
225	315	405	485	525	555
225	315	405	485	525	560
225	315	405	485	525	565
225	315	405	490	530	570
225	315	405	495	540	580
225	315	405	495	545	585
225	315	405	495	550	590
225	315	405	500	555	595
225	315	405	500	560	600

APPENDIX C

Auxiliary Exercise Weight Progression Chart

Set 1	Set 2	Set 3
5	5	5
5	10	10
5	10	15
10	15	20
15	20	25
20	25	30
25	30	35
30	35	40
30	40	45
35	45	50
40	50	55
40	50	60
45	55	65
50	60	70
55	65	75
60	70	80
65	75	85
70	80	90
75	85	95
80	90	100
85	95	105
85	95	110
85	100	115
90	105	120
95	110	125
100	115	130
105	120	135
110	125	140
110	130	145
110	135	150
115	135	155

(continued)

Set 1	Set 2	Set 3
120	140	160
125	145	165
130	150	170
135	155	175
135	160	185
145	170	190
145	175	195
145	175	200
145	175	205
155	185	210
155	185	215
155	190	220
155	195	225
165	200	230
165	205	235
175	210	240
175	215	245
185	220	250
185	225	255
185	230	260
195	235	265
195	240	270
205	245	275
205	245	280
205	245	285
205	255	290
205	255	295
215	265	300
215	265	305
225	275	310
225	275	315

APPENDIX D

Personal Best Conversion Chart

				Number of repetitions					
10	9	8	7	6	5	4	3	2	1
115	115	120	120	125	130	135	140	145	150
115	120	125	130	135	140	145	150	155	160
125	130	135	140	145	150	155	160	165	170
135	140	145	150	155	160	165	170	175	180
145	150	155	160	165	170	175	180	185	190
155	160	165	170	175	180	185	190	195	200
160	170	175	180	185	190	195	200	205	210
170	180	185	190	195	200	205	210	215	220
175	185	190	195	200	205	210	215	220	230
185	195	200	205	210	215	220	225	230	240
190	200	205	210	215	220	230	235	240	250
200	210	215	220	225	230	240	245	250	260
205	215	220	225	230	235	245	250	260	270
215	220	230	235	240	245	255	260	270	280
225	230	235	240	245	250	260	270	280	290
235	240	245	250	255	260	270	280	290	300
240	250	255	260	265	270	280	290	300	310
245	255	260	265	270	280	290	300	310	320
255	265	270	275	280	290	300	310	320	330
260	270	280	285	290	300	310	320	330	340
270	275	285	290	300	310	320	330	340	350
275	280	290	295	305	320	325	340	350	360
280	285	295	305	315	330	335	345	355	370
290	295	305	315	325	340	345	355	365	380
300	305	310	325	335	350	355	360	375	390
310	315	320	330	345	355	365	375	385	400
315	325	335	345	355	365	375	385	395	410
325	335	345	355	365	375	380	390	405	420
335	345	355	365	375	385	395	405	415	430
345	355	365	375	385	395	405	415	425	440
355	365	375	385	395	405	415	425	435	450
360	370	380	390	400	415	425	435	445	460
365	385	395	405	415	425	435	445	455	470

(continued)

				Number of repetitions					
10	9	8	7	6	5	4	3	2	1
370	390	405	415	425	435	445	455	465	480
380	400	415	425	435	445	455	465	475	490
385	410	420	430	445	455	465	475	485	500
400	420	430	440	455	465	475	485	495	510
405	425	435	450	460	475	485	495	505	520
410	430	440	455	465	480	490	500	515	530
415	440	450	465	475	490	500	515	525	540
425	450	465	475	490	500	515	525	535	550
435	460	475	485	500	515	525	535	545	560
440	470	480	490	505	525	535	545	555	570
445	475	485	500	510	530	540	555	565	580
455	480	495	510	525	535	550	565	575	590
460	480	500	515	530	545	555	575	585	600

Glossary

active rest—The strength-training period in which the athlete allows the body to recuperate by reducing the amount of strength training performed or doing other physical activities to maintain strength.

auxiliary exercise—Exercise that works a specific muscle or group of muscles to complete total body strength or to isolate a specific muscle area.

collar—A clamp that secures the plates to the bar.

contraction—The reaction of the muscle as it works against a resistance; shortening of the length of a muscle.

cool-down—Easy exercises to bring body back to pretraining status.

core exercises—Exercises that work the main muscle groups and serve as a base for all strength-training programs.

double pyramid—Extra sets using progressively less weight that an athlete performs after working the heaviest weights.

estimated personal best—The approximate equivalent for one repetition max (1 RM) calculated by using the weight performed for several reps along with a formula.

explosive movement—Movement done vigorously for a very short duration.

flexibility—The athletic ability to extend, move, or rotate body parts in a full range of motion.

free weights—Barbells and dumbbells that can be used many ways without restrictions.

frequency—The number of times per week, day, or season an athlete trains.

full range of motion—The greatest range of movement a muscle or body part can achieve.

hypertrophy—The increased size of muscle gained through exercise or strength training.

in-season training—Strength training performed during the competition season to maintain strength levels.

intensity—How heavily an exercise is performed.

isolate—To zero in on a specific muscle.

joint stability—The strength of a body joint due to strength training.

lift-off—Help given by a spotter (partner) to unrack the bar.

load—The amount of weight (resistance) an athlete is using during exercise execution.

lower body exercises—Strength-training exercises that work the main muscle groups of the lower body.

manual resistance—Exercises done while a partner applies resistance.

max—The heaviest weight an athlete can lift in a particular exercise.

muscle fatigue—Condition of the body after strenuous training.

muscular balance—The maintenance of the natural strength ratio between opposing muscle groups.

off-season training—The period during which the athlete is not in sport competition but is strength-training to bring strength to a higher level.

overtraining—A point at which the athlete reaches a plateau or reduction in performance of strength training.

power—The ability of a muscle to contract forcefully and exert maximum force.

preseason—The strength-training period just before the sport season begins, in which the athlete should be at his optimal strength level.

prescribed workout—The workout assigned to

the athlete, which includes the exercise, weight, sets, and reps.

progressive resistance—A system of strength training that progressively and gradually increases the resistance (weight) the athlete uses toward greater strength gains.

pyramid system—A strength-training program in which the athlete performs a number of sets with increasing weight loads and decreasing repetitions.

repetitions maximum (RM)—The maximum weight that can be used for a specific number of repetitions.

recovery—The time necessary for muscles to recuperate after a workout.

repetitions (reps)—The number of times an exercise movement is repeated.

resistance—The weight the athlete uses to perform the exercise.

rest—The period of training inactivity between sets or workouts to allow for muscle recovery.

set—A group of repetitions of the same exercise and weight.

split routine—A program that works half the body parts on one day and the other half on another day.

spotters—The assistants who stand by to help the athlete in the event of an unsuccessful attempt, to offer encouragement, and to maintain safety.

spotting techniques—Variations of spotting depending on the exercise performed.

strength level—How strong an athlete is, based on the length of time the athlete has been training.

strength-training techniques—The proper method of performing an exercise to improve strength and to avoid injury.

testing—The period in which an athlete's strength progress is evaluated.

total-body routine—A strength-training routine that trains the total body on each workout day.

variable resistance machines—Machines consisting of cams or leverages that can change the actual resistance throughout the full range of motion.

volume—The total work performed during training per workout, week, or season.

warm-up sets—Exercises an athlete performs with lighter weights before exercising with heavier weights.

weight progression—A systematic way of increasing the weight from one set to the next.